P9-DMK-492

SUSHI

The Beginner's Guide

Created by Penn Publishing Ltd.

Published by Imagine Publishing, Inc.
25 Whitman Road, Morganville, NJ 07751
and Penn Publishing Ltd.
1 Yehuda Halevi Street, Tel Aviv, Israel 65135

© 2009 by Penn Publishing Ltd.

ISBN 13: 978-0-9822939-6-6
ISBN 10: 0-9822939-6-8
Library of Congress Control Number: 2009922016

2 4 6 8 10 9 7 5 3

Printed in China
All rights reserved

For information about custom editions, special sales,
premium and corporate purchases, please contact
Imagine Publishing, Inc. at specialsales@imaginebks.com

SUSHI
The Beginner's Guide

Aya Imatani

PHOTOGRAPHY BY MOSHE COHEN

Contents

INTRODUCTION **7**

THE BASICS **12**

Tools for the Sushi Master (or Mistress) 14

Tableware 17

The Japanese Pantry 19

In a Pickle: How to Make Pickled Ginger 23

The Wonders of Wasabi 23

FISH AND SEAFOOD **24**

How to Choose a Whole Fish 26

Glossary 28

Choosing a Fillet 31

You Can Do It! How to Fillet a Whole Fish 31

SAUCES **34**

How to Make Sushizu 36
Sushi Vinegar

Tsukuri Jyouyu 37
Special Soy Sauce for Sashimi

Karashisumiso Sauce 37

Teriyaki Sauce 38

Spicy Sauce 39

SASHIMI **40**

Introduction 42

How to Slice a Fillet for Sashimi 43

Sashimi Vegetables 44

Arranged Maguro Sashimi 46
Tuna

Sake Sashimi 47
Salmon

Kawa Suzuki Arai 48
Freshwater Bass

Takosumiso 49
Sliced Octopus

SUSHI RICE **50**

NIGIRI **54**

Maguro Nigiri 57
Tuna

Ebi Nigiri 58
Shrimp

How to Boil & Butterfly Jumbo Shrimp 59

Unagi Kabayaki Nigiri 60
Steamed & Teriyaki-Broiled Eel

How to Prepare Unagi Kabayaki 61
Teriyaki-Broiled Eel

Tamago Nigiri 62
Japanese Omelette

Dashimaki Tamago 62
How to Make a Japanese Omelette

Arranged Tamago Nigiri 63
Japanese Omelette

GUNKANMAKI **64**

Ikura Gunkanmaki 66
Salmon Roe

Ebikko Gunkanmaki 67
Shrimp Roe

Maguro & Uzaru Gunkanmaki 68
Tuna and Quail Egg

Spicy Tuna Gunkanmaki 69

Grilled Tuna Salad Gunkanmaki 70

Spicy Shrimp Gunkanmaki 71

Negi Shima-Aji Gunkanmaki 72
Yellowjack & Scallion

Kani & Ebikko Gunkanmaki 73
Shrimp Roe & Crab

Kani & Ebikko Salad 73
Shrimp Roe & Crab Salad

TEMAKI **74**

Unatama Temaki 76
Broiled Eel, Tamago & Seasoned Shitake Mushroom

Seasoned Shitake Mushroom 76

Negi Maguro Temaki 78
Scallion & Tuna

California Temaki 79
Shrimp, Crab Salad & Asparagus

Hokkai Temaki 80
Salmon, Avocado, & Cucumber

Norwegian Temaki 81
Salmon, Grilled Salmon & Salmon Roe

HOSOMAKI **82**

Tekka Maki 84
Tuna

Ebikyu Maki 85
Shrimp & Cucumber

Unakyu Maki 86
Eel & Cucumber

Sake Maki 87
Salmon

Hokkai Maki 88
Salmon & Avocado

Tamago Maki 89
Japanese Omelette

SAIMAKI **90**

Magurotaku Saimaki 92
Tuna & Pickled Radish

California Saimaki 94
Shrimp, Asparagus & Cucumber

Norwegian Saimaki 96
Salmon, Avocado & Scallion

Futomaki 98
Shrimp & Broiled Eel

ALL-VEGETARIAN SUSHI **100**

Shitake Maki 102
Shitake Mushrooms

Oshinko Maki 103
Pickled Radish

Saishoku Saimaki 104
Mixed Vegetables

Aspara Maki 106
Asparagus

Kappa Maki 107
Cucumber

JAPANESE SOUPS **108**

Misoshiru 110
Miso Soup

Suimono 112
Fish-Flavored Clear Soup

KAWARIZUSHI **114**
Aya's "Specials"

Ohinasama Chirashi 116
Salmon & Broiled Eel

Youfuu Oshizushi 118
Salmon

Sushi Cake 120
Chicken & Cashew Nut Teriyaki

Temarizushi 122
Tuna, Salmon & Avocado

Saladmaki 124
Jumbo Shrimp & Lettuce

INDEX **126**

In loving memory of my parents,
Ryoko & Keizo Imatani, who
gave me my first exciting taste
of sushi.
And to my husband Srul and
daughter Danielle Ryoko–who
share my love of sushi today.

Introduction

When I first visited New York, I felt like I was walking into "Sushi City." Uptown. Downtown. There was sushi all over town—in restaurants, bars, groceries, fancy gourmet shops, corner delis, and even tiny take-out joints. There they were—those ***little black-bottomed plastic trays*** *with the same clear covers filled with an assortment of sushi—some looking fresh and enticing, and some looking downright dry and unfriendly. Ick!*

"Do people also make their own sushi?" I asked my friend Oscar, and he just laughed. "No way," he said. "Sushi is In, gorgeous, delicious, but you have to be a sushi master to make it! I don't know anyone who would dare make sushi at home—except you, Aya!"

So, okay, I have always made sushi at home. And it surprises me that people think it's so complicated. True, there are sushi masters out there who study the art of sushi for decades. But you don't have to be Julia Child to make a peanut butter and jelly sandwich, right? So why can't regular people make sushi?

Sushi really can be as simple as PB & J. Even for people afraid of raw fish, there are many varieties of sushi that incorporate only vegetables or even cooked ingredients. In this book, you'll learn all the basics for all these varieties, step-by-step, just as if I'm standing there alongside of you.

And who am I? Not just someone who learned to make sushi at home and is now writing a book about it—anybody could do that! Sushi has been a part of my life since infancy. My father owned a sushi bar in Kobe, Japan, and while other children were playing with blocks, I filleted my first fish at the age of five! Owning a sushi bar was a demanding business, and when my brother and I were little, our parents were often busy. But every night, after closing time, the two of us sat down at the bar just like grownups and Otosan (Father) made us whatever kind of sushi we asked for. Now that I've grown up and work in the restaurant business, I can really appreciate that special attention. For us, it made the hours of waiting worthwhile, and created a love and respect for sushi I still feel to this day.

When I was little, sushi bars in Japan were

very expensive (some still are!), so most people would only go there to celebrate a birthday, anniversary, or special event. The truth is that most Japanese people are still a bit hesitant to go into a traditional sushi bar and order a la carte (mainly because the price list is nowhere in sight!). You could ask the sushi chef, but it isn't considered "cool" to ask. Actually, the managers of sushi bars are in favor of price lists, but some customers object, for fear that they might look "cheap." Since many of them are taking out business clients, if the food is good and the mood is congenial, the price is right no matter what it is. So until recently, sushi bars in Japan were not places that students or young couples frequented like they do in America. Lucky you!

And lucky for the Japanese, the state of things in Japanese sushi bars has changed drastically since the invention of kaitenzushi bars, what you might call the hi-tech answer to sushi-for-everyone. In a kaitenzushi bar, the sushi is placed on plates on a conveyor belt, that runs all around the place. The color of the plate depends on the ingredients, and each color has a different price. "I'll take one of 100 yen, and two of 150," you might say, depending on how much you want to spend. And that's quite a relief, considering the alternative! Today, kaitenzushi bars are everywhere, and since there's so much competition, owners know that if the sushi isn't fresh or if there's not enough variety, there's another bar just around the corner. When the first kaitenzushi bar was introduced, everyone was skeptical. Now they can eat their hat, and we can eat our sushi!

But don't think traditional sushi bars have disappeared from Japan entirely. There are still those who have been in business for over fifty years. You'd be amazed at the elegance of the food served at these classic sushi bars, and the truth is that the taste and aesthetics can't be beat. There you can enjoy the harmony of the finest ingredients and the best culinary skills Japan has to offer. If you're visiting Japan, don't miss this experience!

Today, I run a Japanese catering business, and I've served sushi to many people in many places throughout the world. But because I live outside Japan, most of my clients aren't Japanese. Do I serve different sushi to Japanese clients? Yes and no. It's important to me to get the best of what's in season for all my clients, and I try to give my Japanese clients the kind of sushi that they can't get in restaurants or bars. But I've also discovered that, while the Japanese like their sushi arranged with elegant simplicity, many non-Japanese people look at the same "elegant simplicity" as a half-empty plate! One of the greatest things about making your own sushi is that it lets you develop your own personal style and aesthetics. So, just as I develop my sushi menus to fit my clients, you too should let your imagination soar as you learn from this book!

Is sushi healthy? Science has shown that seaweeds do contain impressive amounts of protein, calcium, B complex vitamins, the antioxidant vitamin A, and other vitamins and trace minerals (especially nori), in addition to everything we put on the sushi rice... But Japanese food can also be unhealthy if you choose poor ingredients or use too much sugar, salt, or oil. So remember—whatever you eat may be good for you or not, depending on the ingredients, the way you cook them, and even the way you eat.

The Origins of Sushi

Sushi is a very ancient art that was actually created as a way to preserve food.

According to food historians, rice probably originated in Southeast Asia or China, and the people of Thailand and Laos fermented rice and fish as early as 500 B.C. In Japan, the original sushi (beginning in the Heian period, 794-1185 A.D.) used only pickled fish or seafood, and when my ancestors finally did add rice in the 17th century, it was just to help the fermentation process—then the rice was actually discarded! It wasn't until the middle of the Edo period (1700 A.D.) that the ancients discovered the deliciousness of vinegared rice, and which we still enjoy today.

In this book, we'll start with the basics—everything you need to know before you begin: How to choose the right tools and tableware, and what a well-stocked Japanese pantry should have—with clear photos of each of the ingredients, so you'll already feel like a fish-in-water when you're selecting ingredients. Since I firmly believe that only the best and purest ingredients should go into making sushi, I've included easy recipes for how to make your own pickled ginger (it's also a lot less expensive), and even your own genuine wasabi—if you can get your hands on a root.

And to make sure you don't flounder, there are some really important tips on how to choose a whole fish or fillet—so you're sure you're getting the finest and the best. If you're adventurous or do your own fishing, there are even instructions for how to fillet a fish by yourself (that will really impress everyone!), but I'd practice once or twice before doing it before a live audience.

Sauces add lots of flavor to sushi, so next there are easy recipes for everything from sushi vinegar to homemade teriyaki and spicy sauce. Then we move to making different kinds of sashimi, nigiri, gunkanmaki rice balls in nori, temaki hand rolls, thin hosomaki rolls, saimaki (inside-out rolls), and a tempting array of vegetarian sushi, for all you veggie fans (or raw fish-o-phobes) out there.

To accompany your sushi feast, I include recipes for two of the classic soups we Japanese start a meal with. And last, but certainly not least, I include some of the favorite family sushi treats that my mother used to make for the Girl's Day holiday in March, Boy's Day holiday in May, our annual school sports festival in autumn, and other Japanese holidays and special days I remember from childhood.

So go for it, I just know you'll be glad you did.

Enjoy!
Aya

今谷文

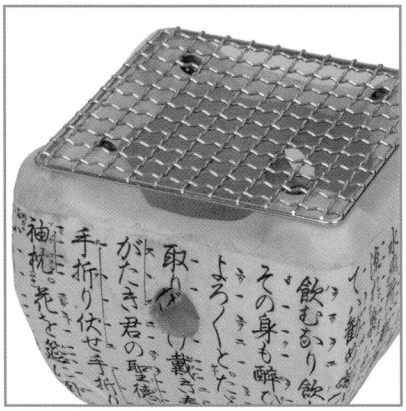
飲むより飲
その身も酔
よろくとた
取り
がたき君の聖
手折り伏せ手折
袖枕。花を

THE BASICS

Tools for the Sushi Master

Having the right tools on hand makes it a lot easier and more enjoyable to make sushi, and while some—like a strainer, bowl, measuring cup, and plastic cutting board—you may already have, there are others that you might have to look for in Asian groceries, health-food stores, and an increasing number of supermarkets. Many are inexpensive, and some are optional. But for best results, the first thing you'll need is a set of authentic Japanese knives (info and tips below).

a. ELECTRIC RICE MAKER
Today virtually everyone in Japan uses an electric rice maker. (In fact, most of them have forgotten how to cook rice without one!) Owning an electric rice maker is helpful, but certainly optional.

b. FINE WIRE MESH STRAINER
(Between 7"-9") for straining cooked vegetables or removing bonito flakes from soup.

c. NORI STORAGE BOX
It's always a good idea to store nori in a storage box to prevent it from absorbing moisture. Use an airtight plastic box, or a metal box with a good seal. Either one works fine.

a

b

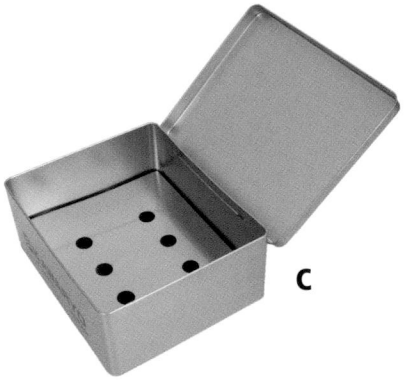
c

g

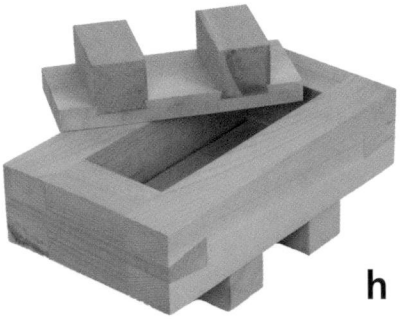
h

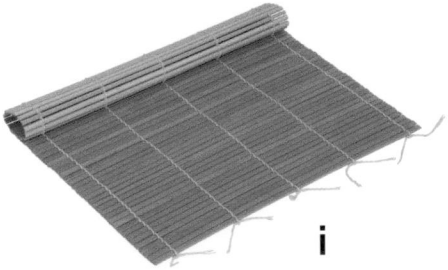
i

d. PLASTIC OR WOODEN BOWL
(Between 12"-15") for mixing rice with vinegar.

e. STAINLESS STEEL BOWL
For mixing sauces.

f. HONENUKI
Tweezer to remove fish bones.

g. HIBACHI
A compact little barbeque, used with charcoal for broiling seafood, and grilling eel, salmon or tuna.

h. FRAME
For making Youfuu Oshizushi (p. 118).

i. MAKISU
STANDARD BAMBOO SUSHI MAT
Although two kinds are sold, you want the type made with flat slats, usually green on one side. After using, brush out any stray pieces of rice. Rinse under running water with a little soap if desired, and dry thoroughly before storing. Never put a sushi mat in the dishwasher!

j. TEMAKI-YOU MAKISU
SUSHI MAT FOR TEMAKI (hand rolls)
About 5" x 5". Instructions for care are the same as for standard bamboo sushi mat. Wooden sushi paddle for transferring rice to hand roll.

k. TOISHI
Japanese knife sharpener. This is the best type of sharpener to sharpen Japanese knives. Always keep the stone submerged in water. (For best results, change water every week.)

l. KITCHEN TOWELS
Made of polyester, perfect for drying knife and wiping hands while working. Unlike terry towels, these towels do not leave fibers on the food or work surface.

d

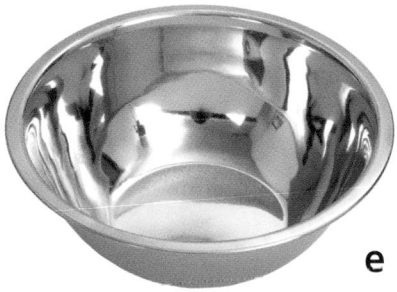
e

f

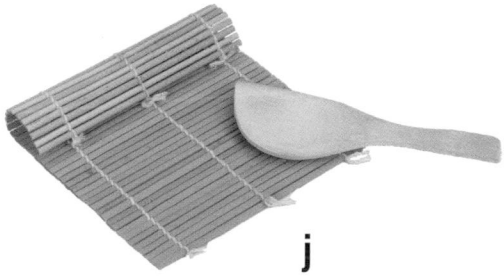
j

k

l

m. MANAITA
PLASTIC CUTTING BOARD
Recommended size: 20" x 10", at least 1" thick. To avoid bacterial contamination, wipe with a little diluted bleach and place in the dishwasher.

n. GLASS SHAKERS
For Shichimi (Japanese chili pepper) and Irigoma (roasted sesame seeds).

o. PLASTIC DRESSING BOTTLE
For sauces.

p. JAPANESE KNIVES
Japanese knives are especially designed for the kind of food we want to prepare. Unlike stainless steel knives, authentic Japanese knives are made with a thin carbon steel blade that is sharper than the conventional stainless steel knife, and does less cell damage to the fish when you slice it. Check to see that the blade is firmly attached to the wooden handle. In this picture we see a long Sashimi Bouchou (p 1), used only to slice boneless fillets. A shorter knife (p 2) is the Deba Bouchou—an all-purpose knife for filleting fish or chicken even if it has bones.

There are many different lengths of knives. To choose the right one for you, lift the knife and feel the weight of it in your hand. If it's too heavy, try another one that's lighter. The blade should be about 12" long (without the handle). Wash the blade with soap and water and dry immediately to prevent staining or rust. If you don't use your knife often, oil it lightly and wrap it up in a towel. Store in a dry place.
NOTE: *Japanese chefs never sharpen their knives just before using, because a freshly sharpened knife affects the delicate taste of fish. Always sharpen the day before you intend to use it!*

m

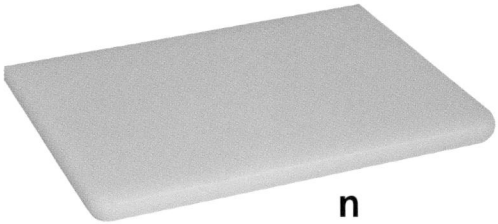
n

o

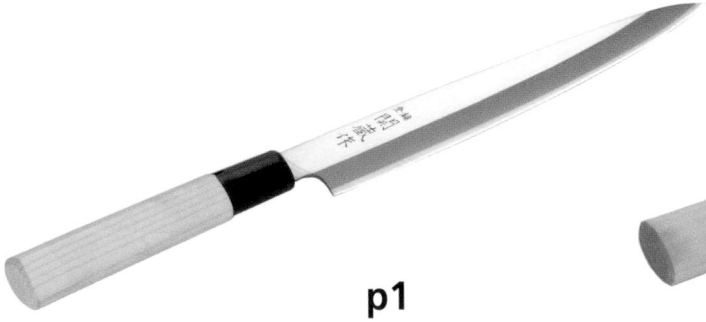
p1

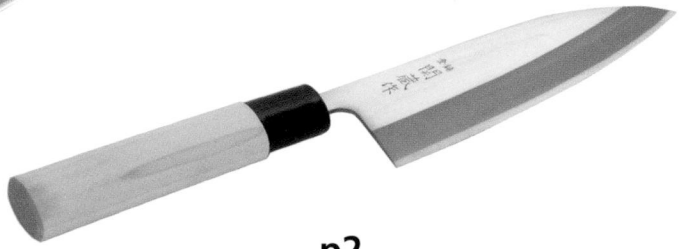
p2

Tableware

Imagine sushi as an actor and the garnish as its costume. The plate is its stage. If you use a plate that's too busy-looking for serving sushi, you won't be able to see or enjoy the sushi clearly.

On the other hand, you don't really need to have a full set of traditional Japanese dishes to serve sushi, but using the right dishes certainly adds to the atmosphere. There are many places to buy Japanese-style tableware, but if you can't find them, use solid-colored plates in interesting shapes like squares or rectangles (circular plates are inappropriate for sushi).

Unlike Chinese food, which is served from a central serving dish, Japanese set the table so that each person has his own utensils—including a placemat and individual soy sauce bowls. And don't crowd the table with flowers; in Japan, we practice Ikebana—the art of flower arranging—using one or two beautiful flowers that make their own statement. Candles are nontraditional.

a. SHOYUZARA
Dish for soy sauce.

b. TAMAKI-DAI
Stand for serving hand rolls.

c. HASHIOKI
Stand for chopstick; Hashi—chopsticks.

d. SUSHIOKE
Traditional lacquer bowl for serving different kinds of sushi.

e. SASHIMIZARA
Dish for sashimi with a separate compartment for soy sauce (ceramic).

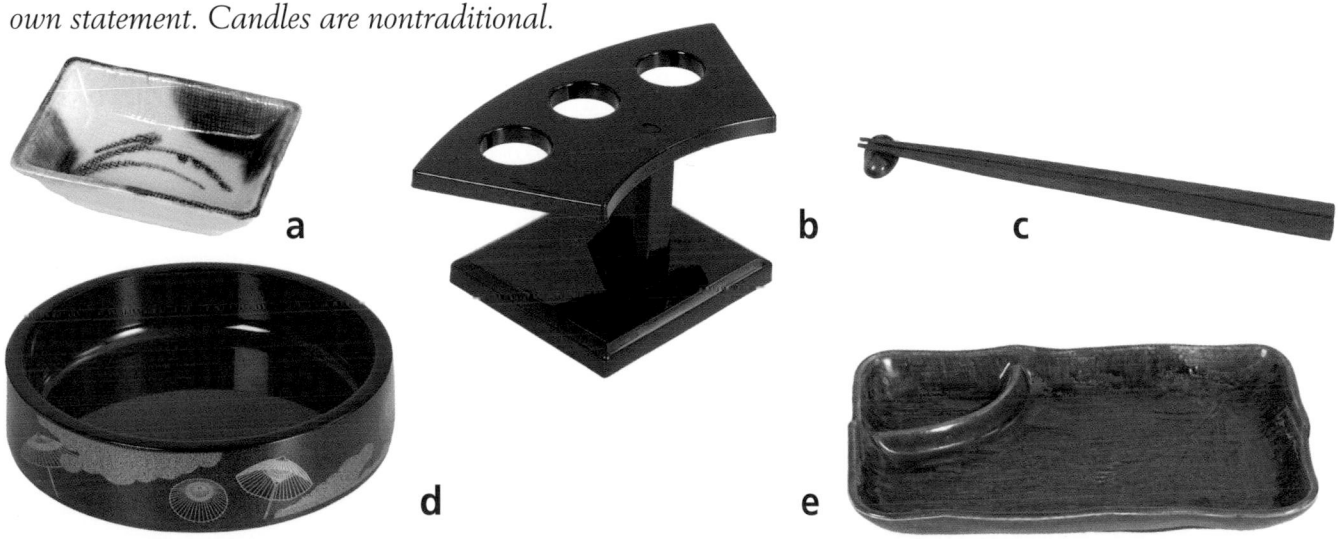

f. JAPANESE APPETIZER PLATE
Can be also be used for serving sushi (ceramic).

g. JAPANESE APPETIZER PLATE
Ceramic.

h. SHIRU-WAN
Wooden soup bowl for miso soup.

i. OCHOUSHI (bottle for sake)
and OCHOKO (cups for sake).

j. YUNOMI
Special green tea cup, for green tea served along with sushi.

k. SHELL CERAMIC DISH
For soy sauce or other condiments.

l. KOZARA (one in front)
& KOBACHI (two in back)
Small dish for salad, arranged sashimi, or condiments like pickles.

m. SASHIMI BUNE
Decorative wooden ship for serving sashimi.

CHOPSTICKS:
Not All Are Created Equal

Chopsticks are the perfect complement to sushi—and wooden ones are the best to use. But not all chopsticks are created equal. The typical Japanese chopstick is 8" long and made of wood, with a thicker top and a thinner bottom. Koreans use the same shape, but made of silver. The Chinese use much thinner and longer (10") chopsticks made of bamboo, lacquered wood, or plastic, and unlike the Japanese, they often use a spoon to eat rice. Thai people use chopsticks shaped like the Chinese version, and frequently eat rice with a fork or spoon. Why the difference?

I believe that the reason lies in the type of rice we eat—both Japanese and Koreans use a sticky type of rice, easy to pick up and transfer to the mouth with two sticks. But Chinese and Thai people eat a drier type of rice, which doesn't have that "adhesive" quality, making it far more practical to use a spoon for rice dishes—and chopsticks for everything else.

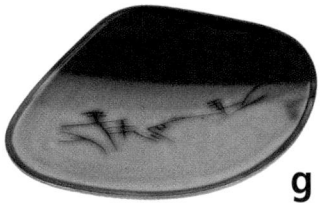

The Japanese Pantry

a. KEZURIBUSHI
Tinted dried bonito flakes, used mostly for soup.

b. NORI
You can judge a quality nori by its color: Good quality nori is black; cheaper kinds are green. To keep fresh after opening, store it in a nori box in a cool place. If you suspect your nori is less than fresh, or if you prefer the taste, toast it by holding the rough side over a flame for just a few seconds. I like to use leftover nori as a sauce for steamed rice: Cook ¼ cup flaked nori, 2 tablespoons mirin, 1 tablespoon sugar, and enough soy sauce to cover the nori over a low flame until thickened. Or cut leftover nori into strips with scissors, and use to garnish soups, fish, or vegetable dishes.

c. UMEBOSHI PLUMS
Small, pink, salted plums used as a condiment. Sold in boxes, bottles, or as a paste, umeboshi plums are believed effective in reducing fatigue, heartburn, and sore throats. Be careful of the pits!

d. GREEN TEA
In Japan, we're always served a big cup of strong green tea when we sit down at a sushi bar. Like pickled ginger, green tea is used to refresh your mouth before eating and between bites. Sushi bars serve a variety of green teas like Sencha (regular green tea), Bancha (coarse green tea), and Konacha (powdered green tea). Sencha is a lightly toasted green tea with a fresher taste than the other types. A fine tea, it is also usually the most expensive. Bancha has a full-bodied flavor, and is moderately priced. While most restaurants serve Konacha tea because of its bright green color, the other types are preferable.

e. MIRIN
Japanese cooking wine made from sticky rice. Store in a cool dark, place after opening. If unavailable, use double the amount of sake and reduce by cooking to the amount required in the recipe.

a

b

c

d

e

f. WAKAME
One of the most popular seaweeds in Japanese cooking, wakame's mild flavor and soft texture make it very suitable for use in salads, soups, and stews. In Japan, we buy it fresh from the fishmonger, but it's much easier to find it dried. To use, reconstitute by soaking in cold water to cover for at least an hour before use.

g. SOY SAUCE
There are many different kinds of soy sauce, but the best one to use for sushi is the Japanese type, of course! Chinese soy sauce is aged for a shorter time than traditional Japanese soy sauce, and may contain additives like sugar.

h. RICE VINEGAR
Rice vinegar is an integral part of sushi rice, and should not be substituted with any other kind of vinegar.

i. TAKUWAN
Pickled daikon (large white) radish. Used in sushi as a condiment or garnish.

j. BLACK SESAME SEEDS
Always toast in a dry frying pan. Use for garnish.

k. JAPANESE MAYONNAISE
Compared to the mayonnaise in other countries, Japanese mayonnaise has a slightly stronger mustard taste. Substitute regular mayonnaise with a little added mustard, if desired.

l. TOFU
A soy "cheese" made from soy beans, water, and a starter, tofu is a low-calorie, low-fat, high-protein food that Japanese call "meat of the field." The quality of tofu depends on the water with which it is made. Once you open the package, store tofu in water to cover, and change daily. Keep refrigerated, and use within three days of opening.

f

g

h

l

m

n

m. MACCHA
Green tea used on special occasions and in the Japanese tea ceremony. Unlike other green teas, this type requires several steps in its preparation, which makes the ceremony that much more impressive!

n. DASHI NO MOTO
Soup stock made of kombu and fish—usually bonito flakes. While you can use many types of fish to make dashi, I never use sardines because of their strong smell and flavor.

o. INARI
Deep-fried tofu pockets (Abura-age) that are cooked with mirin and sake. In Japan, we buy tofu pockets in tofu shops and cook them at home, but they can be found in most Japanese supermarkets.

p. POWDERED SUSHI VINEGAR
An instant product sold in individual sachets, powdered sushi vinegar is very popular in Japanese homes. To make sushi rice, just sprinkle a little on the rice while it's hot!

q. GARI
Pickled ginger is very easy and inexpensive to make at home. See p. 23 for recipe. Ginger is considered one of the oldest and healthiest spices, used in folk medicine throughout the world. In Japan we use ginger peels (from peeling fresh ginger) in tea, or candied in sugar. Try some ginger tea if you feel a cold coming on to soothe a sore throat.

i

j

k

o

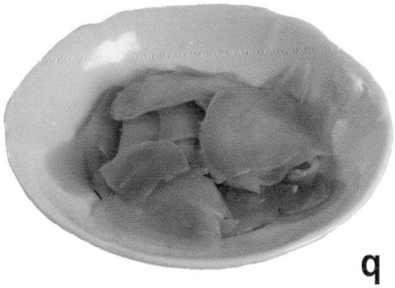
q

r

r. MISO

Miso is a fermented soy bean product with a paste-like consistency. Although it is high in sodium, miso also contains B12 and enzymes beneficial for the digestive system (like yogurt). All types are made with soy beans but some have the addition of wheat or barley. Some are light (like Shiro miso) and some are dark (Aka miso). I always like to mix both dark and light miso in soups. Miso can also be used for making pickles: For real Japanese pickles, make a 1" layer of any kind of miso; a layer of firm vegetables like cucumber, radish, or carrots; and another layer of miso (sometimes mixed with a little mirin or soy sauce). Cover and refrigerate for three days before using. Will keep for up to a week.

s. KAMPYO

A type of Japanese pumpkin or gourd that is available dried in strips or tenderized and already seasoned.

t. DRIED SHITAKE MUSHROOMS

Large dark brown mushrooms that are succulent and almost meat-like in texture. Although fresh shitake mushrooms are available in gourmet stores, we always use dried shitakes for sushi. To reconstitute them, soak in warm water overnight. Remove the stems before use. Shitakes are very healthy— in addition to containing vitamins (like D, B12 and B2) and enzymes, they are considered to having healing qualities. Use leftover water for soups, tempura batter, and cooking fish. The mushrooms can also be used in vegetable stews, soups, sauces, and stir-fries.

u. DRIED KOMBU SEAWEED

Kombu is harvested from the deep, cold water off northern Japan and sun-dried on the beach before packaging. Mostly used for soup stock, reconstituted kombu is also used as a wrap for fish before cooking. Wipe with a towel or brush to remove dust or sand.

r

s

t

u

In a Pickle: How to Make Pickled Ginger

In the best restaurants and sushi bars, we always make our own pickled ginger, but there are many places (and people) that prefer to buy it ready-made. I often find commercial pickled ginger to be too sweet or to have a chemical aftertaste, and you don't want to taint the taste of delicate sushi or sashimi with chemicals, do you?!

It's easy to make pickled ginger at home, but if you buy it ready-made, be sure to check the ingredients on the package before you buy.

GARI (Pickled Ginger)

Always look for fresh ginger that has as thin a skin as possible. The youngest ginger has skin that's almost translucent. Avoid pieces that look dry or shriveled. They will be tough and fibrous inside.

1 pound fresh ginger
2 cups sushi vinegar (see recipe p. 36)
3 tablespoons salt

Wash and dry ginger. Peel and slice as thinly as possible. Discard any sprouted tips. Place ginger in a bowl and mix in the salt. Let stand three minutes. Rinse and drain to remove salt. Transfer to a glass jar and pour over the sushi vinegar. Cover and let stand in a cool dark place (not in the refrigerator) for at least 1 week before using. Taste and add a little sugar if desired. May be stored indefinitely in the refrigerator, but the ginger flavor will deteriorate after long storage.

The Wonders of Wasabi

WASABI POWDER

Wasabi is Japanese horseradish, made from an olive-green root with a bumpy skin. The best roots are more than four years old, which make them quite expensive, even in Japan. Most people outside of Japan use powdered wasabi (which is actually made from a non-Japanese type of horseradish). To make wasabi from powder, add a small amount of boiling water to the powder (using boiling water makes the color very bright and brings out the "heat") and mix well. Let stand until room temperature. Although most people garnish plates with a little "hill" of wasabi, you can also shape it like playdough into a leaf or flower shape. Use within a short time or it will lose its "punch."

WASABI PASTE

There are many brands of wasabi paste, some (but not most) actually containing real wasabi! For best results, use wasabi paste manufactured in Japan. Wasabi paste is always preferable to powder.

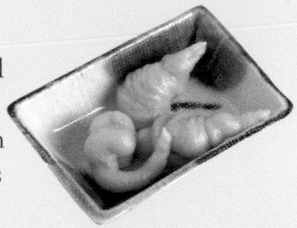

REAL WASABI: BACK TO THE ROOTS

If you should happen to get your hands on a fresh wasabi root, you'll also need a shark's skin board to grind it on. You'll find one in an Asian grocery. Peel the root a couple of inches from the top. Hold the root from the bottom and scrape on the board in a slow circular motion. (It will have a mucilagenous quality.) Never use a grater—the wasabi will lose its heat and be chunky rather than smooth.

In Japan, we never add fresh wasabi to soy sauce like we do in the States. Instead, we put a little minced fresh wasabi on top of the fish, and then dip it in the plain soy sauce.

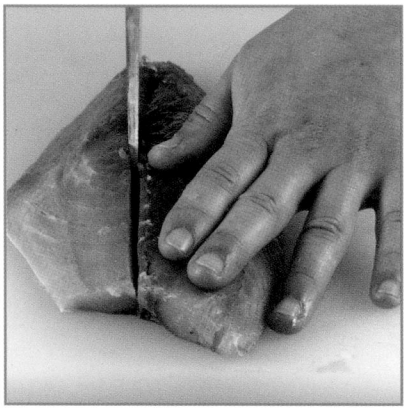

FISH & SEAFOOD

How to Choose a Whole Fish

Many people are wary of buying whole fish because they're afraid of getting stuck with something best fed to their cat. So here's my own tried-and-true method to empower you, so you'll never get stuck with something fishy.

Step 1: Body Language

Check out the body of the fish. This is a good-looking fish; it has no scars or bruises and is moist.

This fish looks like it has seen better days. It is bruised and dry looking, and was probably lying around the shop for up to a week. This kind of fish can be cooked or fried, but should never be used for sushi.

Step 2: The eyes have it!

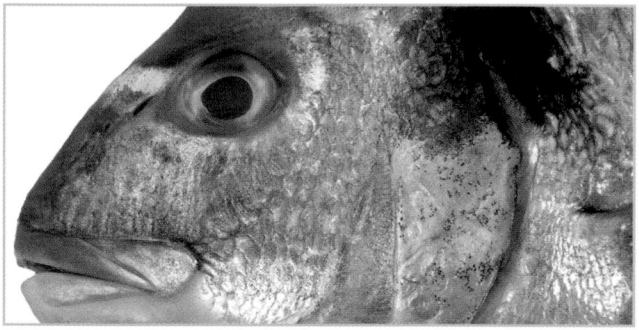

Look at the bright eye on this fish, and see how clear it is. It's perfect!

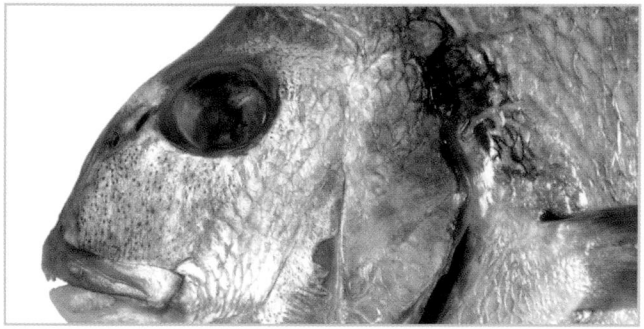

The eye of this fish has already started to turn brown, and it's hard to tell the iris apart from the white. This fish should not be used for sushi, but can still be used for cooked dishes.

Step 3: Check out the fins

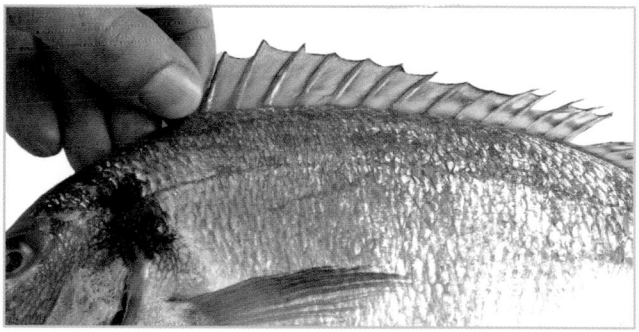

The fins should be moist and undamaged, like on this fish.

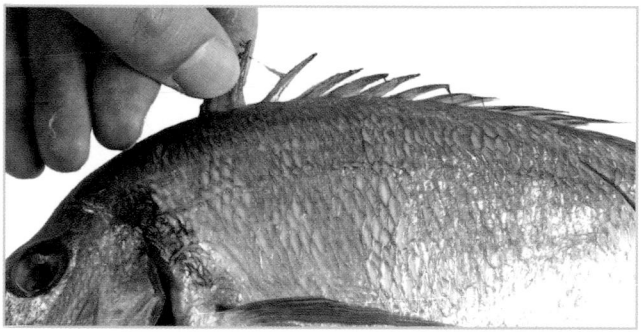

Notice that the fins on this one are separated and broken. This is a fish to avoid!

Glossary

There are an amazing number of fish that can be used to make sushi—but the way they taste not only depends on what kind of fish they are, but also on where and how they were raised. What's the difference?

Throughout my travels around the world, I've discovered that commercially-bred fish just aren't as tasty as those that come from their natural environment—the sea. Sometimes they even have the smell and taste of the food they were raised on. It's amazing! Once I ate farm-raised madai (red snapper) that tasted exactly like sardines, and a friend revealed that the farm it came from indeed fed their fish sardines! In the wild, fish can eat a variety of foods, but farm-raised fish are usually given the same feed everyday. And it makes a difference.

But not only is the feed important; there's even a difference in taste according to climate. For example, the Japanese believe that natural red snapper from a warm climate with mild water currents will never be as tasty as one from a cold sea with wild currents—and that goes for other fish as well.

Incidentally, red snapper could almost be called our Japanese national fish, since it is always served at celebrations. Visually appealing, it is large, beautiful, and pink like a sakura (cherry blossom), mild and noble in taste. We Japanese adore it grilled, cooked and for sashimi.

Since red snapper is also one of my favorite fish, I've tried it all over the world, and while in some places I've enjoyed it immensely, in other places I didn't like it at all! So my advice is to get friendly with a reputable fishmonger and use non-farm raised fish in their natural seasons. And wherever you go, you'll never look like a beginner if you carry this list in your pocket.

AKAMI
RED-COLORED FILLETS

Chutoro (Medium fatty tuna)
In Japan, it is considered a gourmet choice.

Katsuo (Bonito Tuna)
Like a sardine, bonito tuna has a slightly stronger smell and taste. For balance, the Japanese eat it with strong flavors like scallions, ginger, garlic and seasoned soy sauces.

Maguro (Tuna)
This is one of the most popular fish for sushi; low-fat and hi-protein. Yellowfin or bluefin lean cut tuna are the kinds usually used. It's best to experiment with maguro sushi in the winter, when the tuna is at its peak.

Ootoro (Fatty Tuna)
Like french fries, ootoro is very popular among young people and kids because of its oily taste and texture.

HAKARIMONO
SILVERY FISH

All the fish in this category have a slightly stronger smell and taste, so we season or marinate them before using for sushi.

Aji (Horse Mackerel)
Serve with ginger, scallions, a squeeze of yuzu orange or lime juice and soy sauce.

Iwashi (Sardine)
Follow instructions for Aji. Note: Since it's impossible to remove all the tiny bones, only serve this to someone who won't mind! (The bones are rich in calcium anyway.)

Saba (Mackerel)
We never eat mackerel raw. Always salt it first, rinse and marinate in vinegar before serving.

Sayori (Halfbeak)
This fish is the mildest tasting of the group.

NIMONO
STEAMED FISH AND SEAFOOD

Anago (Sea Eel or Sea Conger)
Lighter colored and more delicate flavor and texture than unagi (eel).

Ebi (Shrimp)

Geso (Cuttlefish Tentacles)
A rounder, thicker, and chewier relative of the squid (calamari). Lean and nutritious.

Hamaguri (Large Clam)
Used for nigiri.

Tako (Octopus)

Unagi (Eel)
In Japan, we usually use anago both for sushi and for serving with plain rice. But outside of Japan, people love it for sushi.

SEAFOOD

Akagai (Ark Shell)
One of my favorites!

Ama Ebi (Sweet Shrimp)
Has a slightly sweeter taste. Served raw.

Aoyagi (Surf Clam)
Slightly chewy texture.

Awabi (Abalone)
Always used raw for sashimi and steamed for sushi.

Ebi Odori (Shrimp)
Serve raw.

Ebikko (Shrimp Roe)

Hotate (Scallop)
Mild taste and character.

Ika (Cuttlefish)

Ikura (Salmon Roe)
Orange-red shiny balls. The name ikura derives from "ikra," a word used in Russia and throughout the Mediterranean for fish roe or caviar, or a salad made with it.

Kazunoko (Herring Roe)
Yellow roe chunks, a seasonal winter specialty; somewhat expensive.

Tobikko (Flying Fish Roe)
Tiny bright orange-color eggs, loose and crunchy. Can be prepared as nigiri or maki sushi and is often used for garnishing the outside of rolls.

Torigai (Cockle Clam)

Uni (Sea Urchin)
A delicacy in many parts of the world, uni is actually the gonads of the sea urchin. It has a delicious, subtle, nut-like flavor that is popular among advanced sushi eaters.

SHIROMI
WHITE-COLORED FILLETS

Engawa (Special Fillet of Flounder taken from the stomach area)
Slightly fatty, this is considered a gourmet choice with a special flavor. Consequently, it is also much more expensive than regular flounder fillets.

Hamachi (Yellowtail)
Slightly fatty taste. Look for the smaller fish (or fillets from a smaller fish) because they will be less fatty.

Hiramachi (Amberjack)
Tastes like yellowtail but is far less fatty.

Hirame (Flounder)
One of the best choices for sushi, with a mild taste and almost no smell.

Kurodai (Sea Bream)
Similar to red snapper, but with more tender flesh.

Madai (Red snapper)
One of the best choices for sushi and any Japanese dish.

Shima-Aji (Yellowjack)
Slightly fatty taste. Beware—sometimes Aji (horse mackerel), which is less expensive, is sold as yellowjack (which is more expensive). Make sure you're getting what you pay for!

Suzuki (Sea Bass)
There are both sweet water (kawa suzuki) and saltwater varieties. The saltwater variety is always better.

Choosing a Fillet

Many people buy ready-cut fillets. But how do you know you're not getting a raw deal?

Step 1: Check it out:

Take a look at both these salmon fillets. One was frozen and defrosted, the other one is fresh. Sometimes, disreputable stores will sell frozen fish as fresh. How do you know the difference? The one on the left (which was frozen) has a dull, frosted color, while the fresh fillet on the right has a bright clear color and fibers that can be seen clearly.

Step 2: Check it out:

Now look at these two tuna fillets. The one on the left is very fibrous on the outside. This will be tough and should be avoided. The other one has a nice clear color with no fibers visible. This is the one to choose.

You Can Do It! How to Fillet a Whole Fish

Step 1:

Have the fish scaled and the viscera and stomach removed by the fishmonger. Using a Deba Boucho or other sharp knife, I cut through the flesh just behind the gills, cut or break the backbone at the cut, and remove the head.

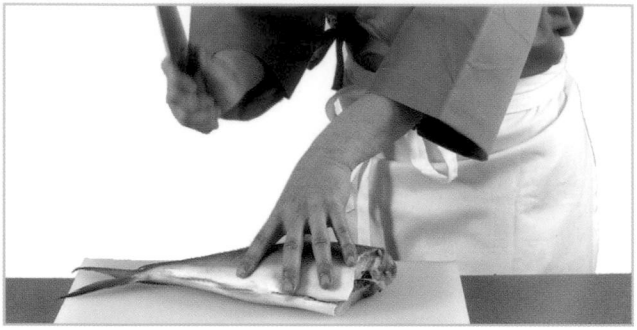

Step 2:

Next, I chop off the tail, and remove the fins on the back and stomach sides, and any small fins near the head.

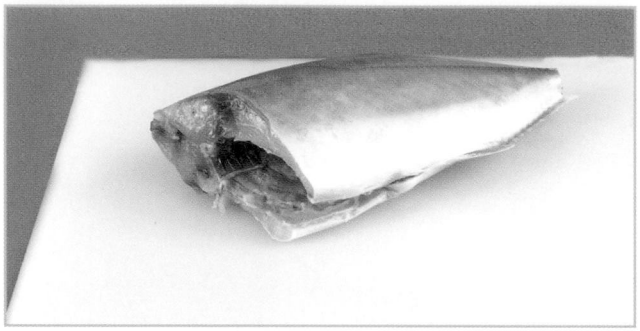

Step 3:

The fish is dressed. (Or undressed. It depends on how you look at it!)

Step 4:

Now we get down to serious business: I place the fish on its side, and insert the knife through the top of the back, and then use the whole blade in gentle sawing motions to cut through one side of the back to the center bone, drawing it down to the middle of the fish.

Step 5:

I turn the fish over and do the same thing starting from the tail side up to the middle. (This will create a single fillet.)

Step 6:

For the other fillet, I repeat step 4, cutting through to the other side of the center bone.

Step 7:

Same as step 5.

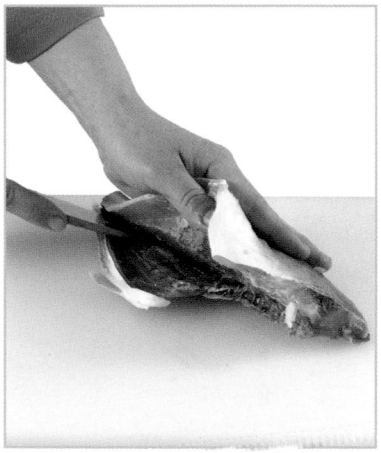

Step 8:

Now I open the fish, skin side down and remove the stomach bone.

Step 9:

With the fingers of my left hand on the back of the fish, and the stomach part facing away from me, I insert the knife and cut the fish from top to bottom, without cutting through the skin.

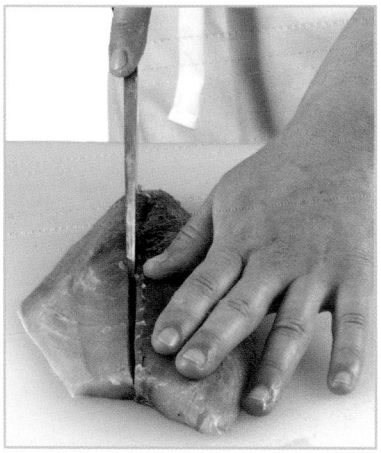

Step 10:

Inserting the knife slightly at an angle, I slide it along the skin to push it away from the center.

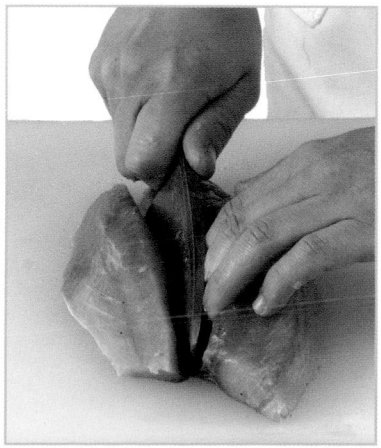

Step 11:

Now that I've removed one fillet, I turn the fish around and remove the other one. Remove any remaining bones in the fillets, wash and pat dry.

Now, wasn't it easier than you thought it would be?!

800 ml
700 ml
600 ml
500 ml
400 ml
300 ml
200 ml
1 1/2 PINT
1 1/4 PINT
1 PINT
3/4 PINT
1/2 PINT
1/4 PINT

SAUCES

How to Make Sushizu

SUSHI VINEGAR

Sushi vinegar "makes" or "breaks" the taste of sushi rice. In fact, another way of calling sushi in Japanese is "shari neta"—"shari" meaning rice, and "neta" meaning fish and seafood. You'll notice the word "rice" comes first, because if you spoil the rice, the fish and seafood will be disappointing!

INGREDIENTS:

4 cups rice vinegar

4 tablespoons sugar

2 tablespoons salt

2 tablespoons sake

1 piece kombu (1" x 3")

1. Pour vinegar, sugar, and salt into a saucepan.

2. Heat on a low flame, stirring constantly with a wooden spoon, just until the sugar and salt are dissolved.

3. Cool to room temperature and add the kombu and sake. Pour into a mason or other jar with a cover. Keep in a cool dark place away from sunlight (refrigeration unnecessary). Keeps indefinitely.

Tsukuri Jyouyu

SPECIAL SOY SAUCE FOR SASHIMI

Although most restaurants serve sashimi with plain soy sauce, in Japan we always serve it with Tsukuri Jyouyu, which is actually a blend of soy sauce and mirin rice wine. The mirin adds a special aroma to the soy sauce, enhancing the taste of the plain fish.

INGREDIENTS:

½ cup mirin

4 cups soy sauce

1 piece kombu (1" x 3")

1. Pour mirin into a saucepan and bring to a boil over high heat. Stir in the soy sauce and bring to room temperature.

2. Pour into a bottle, add kombu, and close tightly. Store in a cool dark place for up to one year.

Karashisumiso Sauce

This is a great sauce for seafood sushi and sashimi, and a typical dressing for steamed vegetable salads. It's really easy to make, and stores indefinitely in the refrigerator.

INGREDIENTS:

4 tablespoons miso (shiro miso is preferable)

1 tablespoon prepared mustard

4 tablespoons sushi vinegar

1 tablespoon yuzu orange (Japanese lime) or lime juice

1. Mix the miso and mustard together and add the vinegar and yuzu orange juice.

2. Beat with a wire whisk until smooth. Pour into a glass jar and store in the refrigerator. Shake before using.

Teriyaki Sauce

Everybody loves Teriyaki sauce, but in Japan, it's far less popular than it is around the world. Actually, "Teri" means shine or glaze, and "Yaki" means grill, which gives you some idea of why and how we use it. Outside of Japan, it's also often used for both marinating and grilling foods, but it can also be used as a dipping sauce. While Teriyaki sauce is sold everywhere, the best and purest kind is always the one you make at home.

INGREDIENTS:

1 cup mirin

1 cup sake

4 tablespoons sugar

1 cup soy sauce (do not use light soy sauce)

1. Pour the mirin and sake into a saucepan and bring to a boil over high heat. Slowly pour in the sugar and stir with a wooden spoon until the sugar is dissolved. Lower heat and cook 1 hour.

2. Add the soy sauce to the pan and continue to cook for an additional 30 minutes over low heat. Pour into a bottle, cover tightly and store in a cool dark place or in the refrigerator.

Spicy Sauce

Spicy sauce is not Japanese. It is a purely American invention that was created especially for those of you who like a little "kick" in your sushi. Some people love this sauce on salads and boiled seafood, chicken, or other mild-tasting foods.

INGREDIENTS:

5 tablespoons Japanese mayonnaise or regular mayonnaise

1 tablespoon tomato paste

1 teaspoon raayu (sesame oil with chili)

A few drops soy sauce or to taste

1. Put the mayonnaise in a bowl and add a few drops of soy sauce.

2. Add tomato paste and mix well.

3. Blend with a wire whisk.

4. Cover and store in the refrigerator, or transfer to a plastic dressing bottle.

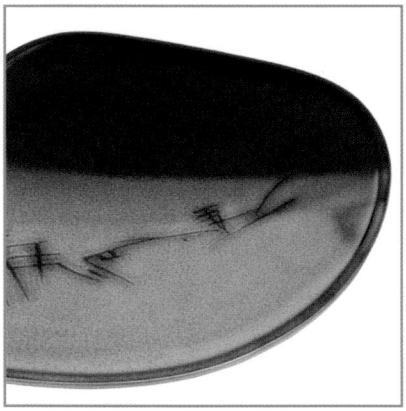

SASHIMI

Introduction

If you ask anyone from Japan what his favorite type of sushi is, he'll answer "Sushi? Not Sushi. Sashimi" because we like sashimi best of all. The word "sashimi" comes from the words "sa" meaning knife and "shi" meaning "fillet", so basically what it is, is just a sliced fillet. You always have to use the best of the best for making sashimi, since the flavors aren't "interrupted" by rice or other ingredients except the sauce or condiment served on the side.

If you were to enter a sushi bar in Japan, you'd almost always see the natives ordering sashimi first, and sushi only afterwards. Sashimi goes especially well with alcohol—and not only sake—like Japanese beer, shouchou (Japanese spirits), or dry white wine.

Outside of Japan, I've frequently seen sushi bars serving freshwater fish just as they would any other kind of sashimi, something you'll never find in Japan! In fact, if I were working in Japan and dared to make a regular sashimi portion from a freshwater fish, I'd lose my job! The reason is, in Japan—where we have become accustomed to such an excellent variety of wild cold salt water fish—people think that raw freshwater fish smells and tastes like mud. Instead of regular sashimi, we prepare it "arai" ("washed")—cutting it as thin as possible, always dipping it in ice water, and serving it with a sauce made of vinegar and miso.

And a word about salmon: Although salmon (sake sashimi) is one of the most popular choices in sushi bars around the world, in Japan it hasn't really caught on until recently. The reason is, that compared with our other wonderful fish, salmon was considered to have a heavy taste and strong odor. When they did make it, Japanese sushi chefs always chose thin slices from the part of the fillet that's near the tail, where it is less fatty and has a milder smell. (It's not that we don't like the taste of fatty fish—it's just that the taste of fatty salmon doesn't appeal to us.)

Tastes have changed in Japan, and today people eat sake sashimi like they do in the rest of the world. In fact, thick slices of fattier salmon called Beni Toro are now more expensive than lean tuna! But when I use salmon for sashimi, I still do what my father taught me—use the tail end of the fillet. You'll also find it's easier to slice thinly.

In this chapter, I'd also like to introduce types of sashimi not typically found in sushi bars. You can't imagine how many ways you can enjoy sashimi!

How to Slice a Fillet for Sashimi

I like to use a Sashimi Bouchou knife for this one, but any good, large, sharp knife will also do.

1. Gently hold the fillet with your left hand. Make sure to curl your fingers under (so they don't become sashimi, too).

2. Cut into 3/8" slices according to recipe directions.

3. This is a typical sashimi platter, with maguro (yellowfin tuna).

Sashimi Vegetables

Sashimi vegetables serve the same function as wasabi or ginger—they refresh your mouth between bites. Decoratively cut, they also add an aesthetic touch to the plate.

The most typical vegetables used to garnish sashimi are radishes (daikon white radish or red radish), (hothouse) cucumbers, lettuce, and fresh shiso leaves, which are sometimes cut into intricate designs. Other possibilities are finely grated carrot, parsley, scallions, and oshinko (pickled radish). Use your imagination, but don't go overboard!

1. For an easy cucumber garnish, hold a small hothouse cucumber on its side, and use a knife to peel off lengthwise strips.

2. Slice the cucumber thickly.

3. For an easy red radish garnish: Slice unpeeled radish very thinly, and line up the slices with edges overlapping.

4. Arrange and serve.

Other garnish possibilities:

a. Ruby loose-leaf lettuce

b. Thinly grated carrots (check out the special grater found in Asian supermarkets)

c. Parsley and julienned radish

d. Thinly sliced hothouse cucumber and carrot crown

e. Oshinko—sliced three different ways

f. Scallions—cut off the root, slice the base into thin lengthwise slices, and place in ice water to curl the bottom into a flower shape.

Arranged Maguro Sashimi

TUNA

This impressive-looking sashimi is really easy to make, once you get the knack of rolling it up. Just remember to overlap the slices, make sure the filling is neatly packed inside, and roll up firmly.

I am also giving you another variation I like, using sake (salmon) and salmon roe. It reminds me of a delicate spring flower.

INGREDIENTS FOR 1 PORTION:

6-8 slices of maguro (tuna) ⅛" thick

8 matchstick slices of oshinko

1 piece nori, 7" x 1"

White sesame seeds (for garnish)

1. Arrange the slices in a line with the edges overlapping. Place the oshinko pieces in a bunch at the beginning of the line. Carefully begin rolling from the bottom up, using your fingers to keep the maguro slices in place. Roll tightly.

2. Wrap a band of nori around the base to keep the sashimi in place.

VARIATION:

Sake Sashimi

SALMON

Here's another variation on the theme, using ten slices of sake sashimi. In this one, I don't use oshinko in the middle: After I roll up the salmon, I carefully fold back the edges, spreading them out slightly like a rose, and fill the middle with about a teaspoon of salmon roe. Garnish with snipped chives and serve on a bed of thinly sliced lemon.

Kawa Suzuki Arai

FRESHWATER BASS

INGREDIENTS:

8-10 slices of suzuki (freshwater bass), cut paper-thin

Ice water

1½ tablespoons chopped scallions (green part only)

Bowl of crushed ice and Karashisumiso sauce for serving

1. Hold the fillet with your left hand, keeping fingers straight instead or curled under. Position the knife on a slight angle (so you don't slice your fingers as well!), and slice the fish paper-thin, using a slight back-and-forth sawing motion.

2. Drop the slices into a bowl of ice water. Use a chopstick to help separate the slices. Let stand for 3-5 minutes. The fillets will shrink slightly.

3. Arrange on top of crushed ice and garnish with chopped scallions. Serve with Karashisumiso sauce.

Takosumiso

SLICED OCTOPUS

In Japan, we prefer to eat octopus steamed in green tea with sake or rice vinegar (sake gives it a milder taste, but vinegar helps the color stay bright). I suggest using Bancha green tea, found in every health food store.

Believe it or not, the octopus that you eat as sashimi in a sushi bar probably came from an octopus about 30" long that weighed more than 10 pounds! Since you probably don't want to deal with such a large octopus in your kitchen, ask your fishmonger to suggest what size of tentacle is necessary for the number of portions you wish to make.

INGREDIENTS FOR 10 TAKOSUMISO PORTIONS:

1 pound cleaned octopus tentacles

Salt

1 Bancha tea bag

4 cups water

1 tablespoon sake or rice vinegar

For serving:

Sliced hothouse cucumbers

Karashisumiso sauce or wasabi and soy sauce

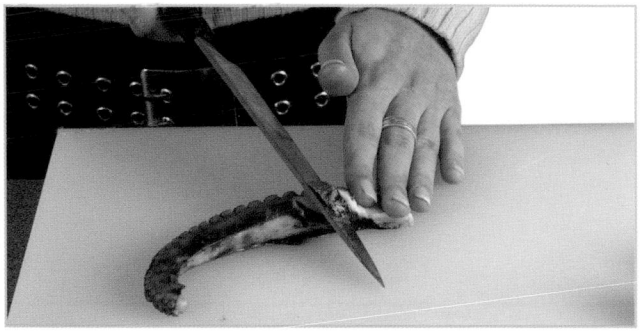

1. Rinse tentacles and massage with salt. Rinse again under running water, paying special attention to the suckers. Place the tea bag, water and sake or vinegar in a large saucepan and bring to a boil. Add the tentacles and cook uncovered over low heat for 10 minutes. Remove the tea bag and let the octopus reach to room temperature in the water. Rinse gently under running water and slice into 1" chunks.

2. Place in a bowl and garnish with sliced cucumbers. Serve with wasabi and soy sauce, or Karashisumiso sauce (my favorite).

SUSHI RICE

Sushi Rice

Now that we've seen how to make sashimi, we move on to sushi—the basis of which is sushi rice, the key to really good sushi. Although as I mentioned before, most people and many sushi bars in Japan use electric rice cookers, I still believe the best way to prepare sushi rice (or any rice for that matter) is by cooking it yourself, especially over a gas burner.

Don't gasp. This recipe makes a lot of sushi rice, but the truth is that it just doesn't have the correct balance of flavors if you make a smaller amount. In Japan, we also take into account that we discard about 15 percent of the cooked rice—especially around the edges and bottom of the pot where the grains are harder. Actually, if you divide the mixture between nigiri, handrolls and other types of sushi, it's the perfect amount for an average dinner or cocktail party, with no rice leftovers.

My father taught me to always buy from this year's stock of rice ("shinmai"), because it will be moister and more flavorful than older rice, and therefore need less water in preparation. If possible, check the package when you buy rice to see if it has the manufacturing date printed on the wrapper. (In some Asian groceries, you can also buy rice by bulk, so make sure to ask for "shinmai").

INGREDIENTS:

4 cups Japanese short-grain (sushi) rice

4 cups water

½ cup sushi vinegar

1. Place rice in a heavy-bottomed pot and rinse with running water.
2. Drain rice.
3. Add 4 cups of water and soak for 30 minutes.
4. Cover with a tight-fitting lid and bring to a boil.
5. Keep cooking on high heat for 15 minutes with lid on.
6. Lower heat to a minimum and cook covered for 10 minutes.
7. Remove from heat, remove lid, and let sit undisturbed for 5 minutes.

Note: *Always moisten your hands in a water-vinegar solution before shaping sushi rice. (See Nigiri tips, p. 56.)*

This quantity of rice can be used for:

110 pieces of Nigiri or Gunkanmaki rice balls in nori

Or 30 Temaki hand rolls

Or 20 thin Hosomaki rolls

Or 12 Saimaki (inside-out) rolls

Or 8 Futomaki (traditional thick) rolls

1. Transfer the hot rice to a large shallow bowl and pour over the sushi vinegar. Now we want the temperature of the rice to cool down quickly so that the grains don't get too sticky. To do that, we fan the rice (today an electric fan on medium speed often replaces the traditional hand fan).

2. As you cool down the rice, use a wooden paddle to gently but constantly fold the mixture, just as you would if you were folding whipped egg whites into a cake batter. Don't stop until the rice cools down to room temperature, or you'll be able to use your sushi rice instead of cement.

3. Here's the finished product. If you've followed the directions correctly, it should have a nice sheen and only be slightly sticky.

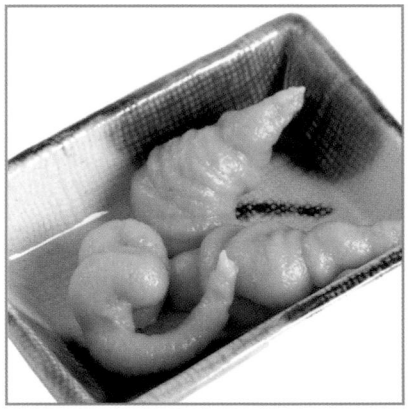

Nigiri

Nigiri

Nigiri, which originated in the city of Tokyo, is the most popular type of sushi ordered in Japanese restaurants, and is always among the sushi selections sold around town. The word "nigiri" means "squeeze" in Japanese, and nigiri is made by gently squeezing small amounts of sushi rice into small rectangular shapes, before topping them with bite-sized pieces of fish or other foods.

The most important thing is to create harmony between the rice and the flavor and size of the topping. In Japan, we also define a good nigiri as one that doesn't fall apart when you transfer it from the plate to your mouth, but is tender when it meets your tongue!

NIGIRI TIPS:

1. Prepare a bowl of water with a 30% rice-vinegar solution to dip your hands in before you pick up the rice. That way, the rice won't stick!

2. Practice makes perfect: Take a ball of rice and squeeze it gently in your hand to form a rectangular shape. Don't squeeze or play around with it too much, or the rice will lose the correct texture. Taste a little and check the firmness of the rice ball; as I mentioned before, it should be tender but not fall apart when lifted.

Here are 4 different kinds of nigiri from left to right:
Kurodai (Sea Bream)
Shima-aji (Yellowjack)
Sake (Salmon)
Maguro (Tuna)

Maguro Nigiri

TUNA

For this nigiri, you can use either yellowfin or bluefin tuna. Bluefin tuna has a meatier texture.

INGREDIENTS FOR 1 PIECE:

1 slightly rounded tablespoon sushi rice

½ ounce yellowfin or bluefin tuna fillet, 2"–3" long, ⅛" thick

1. Moisten hands with water-vinegar mixture. Hold a small ball of sushi rice in your right hand. Squeeze gently into a rectangular shape. Pick up and hold a small fillet of tuna in your left hand.

2. Bring the rice ball to the fillet.

3. Use the thumb and forefinger of your right hand to gently press in the sides of the sushi, and use the thumb of your left hand to gently press it down at the top (which is really the bottom of the upside-down nigiri). Use your right hand to help you turn the pressed nigiri over in your left hand.

4. Now do the same thing—use the thumb and forefinger of your right hand to press in the sides. Use the thumb of your left hand to press the fish and rice together gently. There you have it!

Ebi Nigiri

SHRIMP

INGREDIENTS FOR 1 PIECE:

1 slightly rounded tablespoon sushi rice

1 boiled peeled and butterflied shrimp (recipe follows)

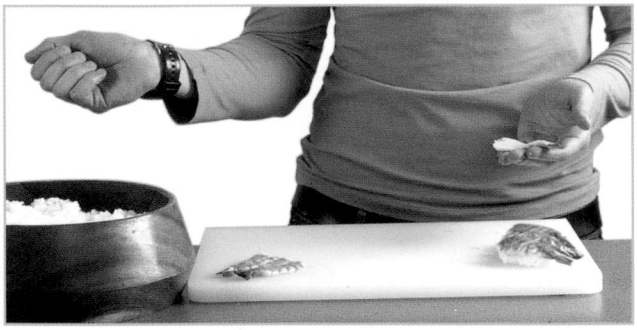

1. Moisten hands in the water-vinegar mixture and pick up a small ball of sushi rice in your right hand. Squeeze gently into a rectangular shape. Pick up and hold a butterflied shrimp in your left hand.

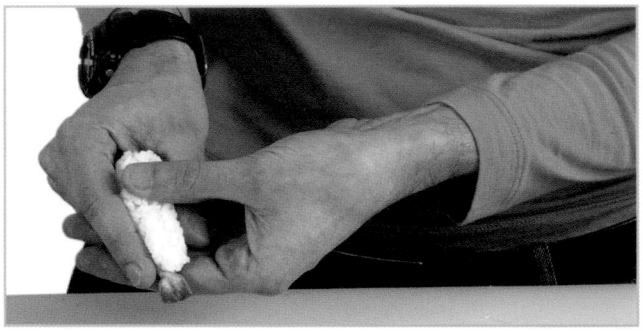

2. Bring the rice ball to the shrimp. Use the thumb and forefinger of your right hand to gently press in the sides of the nigiri, and use the thumb of your left hand to press it down at the bottom (of the upside-down nigiri). Use your right hand to turn the pressed nigiri over in your left hand.

3. Use your thumb and forefinger to press in the sides, and two fingers of your right hand to press the fish and rice gently together st the topside.

4. Here are two kinds of ebi nigiri—with and without a nori band.

How to Boil & Butterfly Jumbo Shrimp

It's really easy to boil and butterfly your own shrimp in just minutes if you follow the process below. You'll note we always skewer the shrimp to help keep it from shrinking and losing its shape.

INGREDIENTS FOR 5 FRESH JUMBO SHRIMPS:

3 quarts water

1 cup rice vinegar

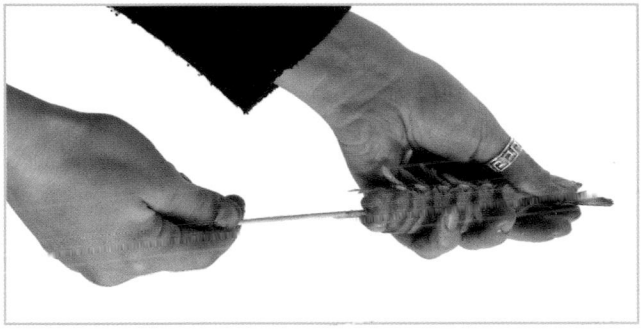

1. Remove the head of the shrimp and insert a long bamboo skewer through the middle—starting from the top and working it through in the direction of the tail. Use your thumb to press and flatten the center of the tail section, to allow more space for the skewer to exit.

2. Bring the water and vinegar to a rolling boil, add the skewered shrimp and cover the pot. Immediately remove from heat, and let stand 3 minutes. Remove the shrimp and let cool to room temperature. Peel the shrimp and set aside.

3. Use a sharp knife (like a sashimi boucho) to slit open the inner edge from top to bottom, making sure not to cut all the way through. Gently open the shrimp and flatten.

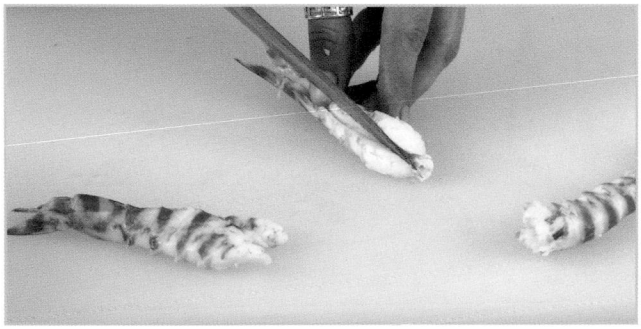

4. Repeat with the remaining shrimp.

Unagi Kabayaki Nigiri

STEAMED & TERIYAKI-BROILED EEL

INGREDIENTS FOR 1 PORTION:

1 slightly rounded tablespoon sushi rice

3"– 4" long, 1" wide piece broiled unagi (recipe follows)

1 band nori 4" long, ½" wide

1. Moisten hands with a water-vinegar mixture. Hold a small ball of sushi rice in your right hand. Squeeze gently into a rectangular shape. Pick up and hold a small fillet of eel in your left hand.

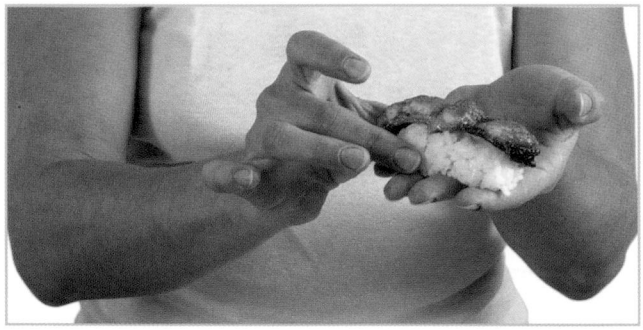

2. Use your right hand to place the unagi fillet on the rice (to avoid getting your hands dirty from teriyaki sauce).

3. Place the nori band around the nigiri. Help them stick to each other by lightly moistening the edges of the band.

4. Here are two kinds of Unagi Kabayaki Nigiri—with and without a nori band.

How to Prepare Unagi Kabayaki

TERIYAKI-BROILED EEL

To begin:

Put the sticks through the widthwise side of the fillet 2" apart from each other. Cover and steam in a steamer basket placed over boiling water for 10 minutes. Remove and bring to room temperature. (Do not remove the skewers.)

INGREDIENTS:

1 x 10" long fresh eel fillet

5 bamboo skewers

1 cup teriyaki sauce (see my recipe p. 38)

1. Here's what the fillet looks like after steaming. Note the color. Place the eel in a glass or non-reactive baking dish and brush with teriyaki sauce. Grill over low coals (or on a hibachi) for 3-5 minutes, brushing with teriyaki sauce each time the fillet looks dry (which is often).

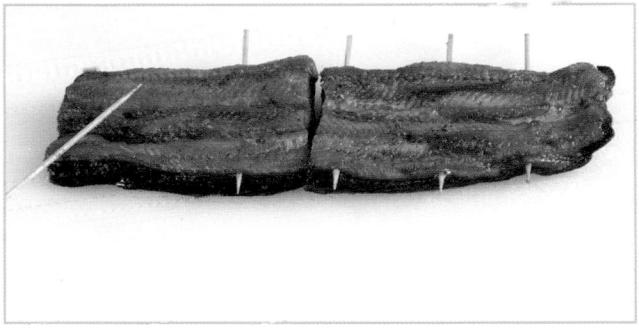

2. Here's what the fillet looks like after grilling. It should be shiny and glazed on top. Check out the color.

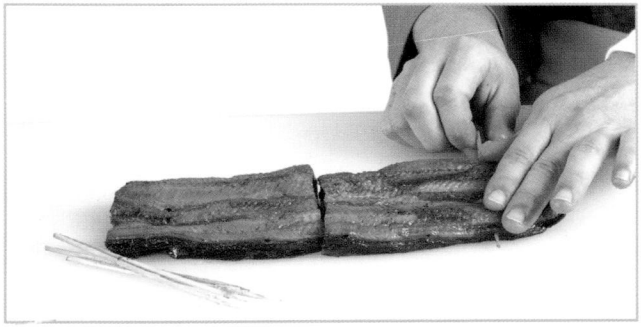

3. Gently remove the skewers from the fillet.

4. Slice widthwise into 1" pieces.

Tamago Nigiri

JAPANESE OMELETTE

The original tamago (Japanese omelette) was nothing like the sweet omelette served in sushi bars today. Made of white-meat fish pureed with eggs, mirin, sake and bonito flakes—it had a different texture and only a very delicate sweetness.

For this nigiri, I include a recipe for a modern tamago that uses dried bonito flakes instead of fresh fish, and is still far closer to the original version than anything you'll find in your local sushi bar (recipe follows).

INGREDIENTS FOR 1 PIECE (with nori band):

1 ½ slightly rounded tablespoons sushi rice

1 slice of tamago omelette (3"– 4" long, 1 ½" wide, ¼" thick)

1 band nori, 4" long, ½" wide

Moisten hands with water-vinegar mixture. Hold a small ball of sushi rice in your right hand. Squeeze gently into a rectangular shape. Pick up and hold a slice of tamago in your left hand, and bring the rice to the tamago. Use your right hand to turn the pressed nigiri over in your left hand. Now place the nori band on top and fasten the edges under the rice. Arrange on a serving plate and garnish with wasabi and ginger.

Serve either or both kinds of Tamago Nigiri with wasabi and ginger.

How to Make Dashimaki Tamago (Japanese Omelette)

The traditional Japanese omelette pan is an impressive-looking 9" square made of copper, but in homes today, most people use a 7" x 5" rectangular Teflon-coated one. If you don't have one, use a 10" round skillet and trim the edges of the omelette once it's cooked.

Since the process of making a real tamago is a little tricky, you might want to make "crepes" ½" thick, trim the edges, and fold them as outlined in Step 10.

NOTE: Tamago omelettes can only be cooked over a gas stove. If yours is electric, give these instructions to a friend (or buy ready-made tamago).

INGREDIENTS FOR A 5" LONG, 3" WIDE, 1" HIGH OMELETTE (20 Nigiri portions):

6 large eggs

¼ cup water

2 tablespoons sake

1 tablespoon kezuribushi (dried bonito flakes) or 1 teaspoon dashi no moto

1 ½ tablespoons sugar

2 – 3 drops soy sauce

Corn or sunflower oil for frying

Arranged Tamago Nigiri

JAPANESE OMELETTE

This attractive-looking Tamago Nigiri is traditionally made with a pinch of sakura denbu (sweet cod powder) on top for garnish.

INGREDIENTS FOR 1 PIECE:

1 ½ slightly rounded tablespoons sushi rice

1 slice tamago 3"– 4" long, 1 ½" wide, ¾" thick

1 pinch sakura denbu, for garnish

1. Moisten hands with water-vinegar mixture. Using a sharp knife, cut the tamago lengthwise down the center, but not all the way through.

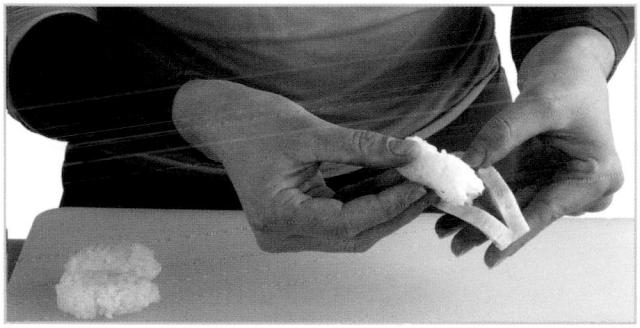

2. Make a small ball of sushi rice in your right hand. Squeeze gently into a rectangular shape. Gently place the nigiri rice in middle of Omelette. Garnish with a pinch of sakura denbu.

1. Place water and sake in a saucepan and bring to a boil over high heat.
2. Add kezuribushi, stir, and remove from heat.
3. Strain through a wire-mesh strainer and discard the kezuribushi.
4. Add sugar to the water-sake (dashi) mixture and mix well until dissolved. Bring to room temperature.
5. In a bowl, whisk together eggs until light and fluffy.
6. Add cooled dashi and few drops of soy sauce and mix well.
7. Strain the egg-dashi mixture so it is very smooth.
8. Lightly grease the omelette pan and heat over medium heat.
9. Pour just enough egg-dashi mixture into the pan to form a thin crepe. Use chopsticks to press out any air bubbles.
10. When slightly dry on the top, run chopsticks around the edges to loosen them. Now comes the tricky part: Imagine the omelette is divided by horizontal lines into thirds – the first third being the farthest away from you. Use chopsticks to fold ⅓ of the omelette from the far side towards the center. Now fold these two-thirds in your direction over the remaining ⅓.
11. Pour a little more egg-dashi mixture in the empty side of the pan, lifting the cooked omelette to let it flow underneath.
12. Repeat Step 11 and then Step 10 until tamago is 1" thick.
13. Remove tamago from pan and tighten with a bamboo sushi mat (makisu). Let chill to room temperature, and remove the makisu.
14. Cut into strips.

GUNKANMAKI

Personally, I think the name of this sushi is kind of weird, since "Gunkan" means battleship, which is kind of a funny name to use for sushi. But actually, this oval rice ball with nori wrapped around it does look a little like a boat, but I prefer to think of it as a sailboat – sailing off to some exotic destination.

Ikura Gunkanmaki

SALMON ROE

INGREDIENTS FOR 1 PORTION:

1 slightly rounded tablespoon sushi rice

1 gunkan nori band (⅛ sheet=7" x 1")

1 teaspoon salmon roe

2 thin slices hothouse cucumber, cut in half

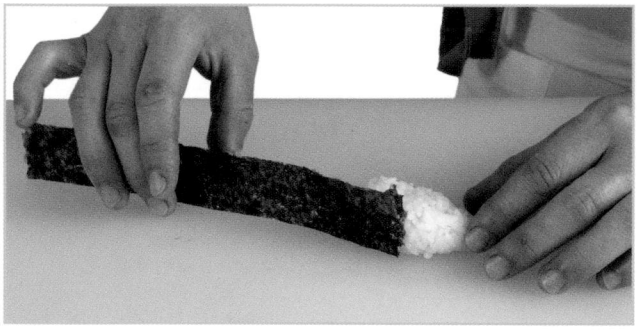

1. Moisten hands with water-vinegar mixture. Hold a small ball of sushi rice in your right hand. Squeeze gently into a rectangular shape just like you did for nigiri. Place on a work surface. Attach one end of the nori to the middle of the rice ball.

2. Keep wrapping the nori around, making sure to keep it equidistant from the bottom.

3. Gunkanmaki is ready for toppings.

4. Stand three of the cucumber half-slices up on the back of the gunkanmaki, and place the ikura on top. Garnish the plate with wasabi and ginger.

Ebbiko Gunkanmaki

SHRIMP ROE

INGREDIENTS FOR 1 PORTION:

1 slightly rounded tablespoon sushi rice

1 gunkan nori band (⅛ sheet=7" x 1")

1 teaspoon shrimp roe

2 thin slices hothouse cucumber, cut in half

1. Moisten hands with a water-vinegar mixture. Hold a small ball of sushi rice in your right hand. Squeeze gently into a rectangular shape, just like you did for nigiri. Place on a work surface. Attach one end of the nori to the middle of the rice ball. Keep wrapping the nori around, making sure to keep it equidistant from the bottom.

2. Stand three of the cucumber half-slices up on the back of the gunkanmaki, and place the shrimp roe on top.

3. Garnish the plate with wasabi and ginger.

Maguro & Uzura Gunkanmaki

TUNA & QUAIL EGG

For those of you unfamiliar with them, quails eggs are tiny brown and white speckled eggs that you can find in gourmet stores and Asian markets.

INGREDIENTS FOR 1 PORTION:

1 slightly rounded tablespoon sushi rice

1 gunkan nori band (⅛ sheet=7" x 1")

1 teaspoon chopped tuna fillet

1 quail egg

1. Moisten hands with water-vinegar mixture. Hold a small ball of sushi rice in your right hand. Squeeze gently into a rectangular shape like you did for nigiri, and place on a work surface. Attach one end of the nori to the middle of the rice ball. Keep wrapping the nori around, making sure to keep it equidistant from the bottom. Now the gunkanmaki is ready for topping.

2. Place chopped tuna on top. Press down center of tuna with your finger.

3. Gently separate the egg, and place the yolk on the center of the tuna.

4. Garnish the plate with wasabi and ginger.

Spicy Tuna Gunkanmaki

INGREDIENTS FOR 1 PORTION:

1½ slightly rounded tablespoons sushi rice

1 gunkan nori band (⅛ sheet=7½" x 1")

1 teaspoon chopped tuna fillet

⅓ teaspoon minced scallion

½ teaspoon of spicy sauce (see recipe p. 39)

1. Moisten hands with water-vinegar mixture. Hold a small ball of sushi rice in your right hand. Squeeze gently into a rectangular shape. Place on a work surface. Attach one end of the nori to the middle of the rice ball. Keep wrapping the nori around, making sure to keep it equidistant from the bottom. Chop the tuna fillet and mince the scallion.

2. Mix the chopped tuna and minced scallion together with your fingers or a chopstick and place on the gunkanmaki. Press down lightly with your finger to flatten.

3. Add spicy sauce on top of gunkanmaki and garnish plate with wasabi and ginger.

Grilled Tuna Salad Gunkanmaki

Unlike for sashimi, you can use a chewier part of the tuna fillet for the salad.

INGREDIENTS FOR 1 PORTION:

1 slightly rounded tablespoon sushi rice

1 gunkan nori band (⅛ sheet=7" x 1")

1½ teaspoons tuna salad (recipe follows)

For the Tuna Salad:

½ cup grilled tuna chunks

⅛ cup thinly sliced onion

2 tablespoons Japanese or regular mayonnaise

1. Prepare the ingredients for Tuna Salad.

2. Mix all ingredients together for the salad.

3. Moisten hands with a water-vinegar mixture. Hold a small ball of sushi rice in your right hand. Squeeze gently into a rectangular shape and place on a work surface. Attach one end of the nori to the middle of the rice ball.

4. Keep wrapping the nori around, making sure to keep it equidistant from the bottom. Gently place 1 teaspoon of prepared Tuna Salad on top of gunkanmaki. Garnish plate with ginger and wasabi.

Spicy Shrimp Gunkanmaki

The winning combination of shrimp, avocado and spicy sauce make this a very popular gunkanmaki.

INGREDIENTS FOR 1 PORTION:

1 slightly rounded tablespoon sushi rice

1 gunkan nori band (⅛ sheet=7" x 1")

1 boiled shrimp, chopped

½ teaspoon chopped avocado

½ teaspoon of spicy sauce (see recipe p. 39)

1. Moisten hands with water-vinegar mixture. Hold a small ball of sushi rice in your right hand. Squeeze gently into a rectangular shape and place on a work surface. Attach one end of the nori to the middle of the rice ball.

2. Keep wrapping the nori around, making sure to keep it equidistant from the bottom. Mix shrimp and avocado together and place on top of gunkanmaki. Pour spicy sauce on top of gunkanmaki.

3. Garnish plate with wasabi and ginger.

Negi Shima-Aji Gunkanmaki

YELLOWJACK & SCALLION

INGREDIENTS FOR 1 PORTION:

1 slightly rounded tablespoon sushi rice

1 gunkan nori band (⅛ sheet=7" x 1")

1 teaspoon chopped yellowjack fillet

⅓ teaspoon minced scallion

1. Moisten hands with water-vinegar mixture. Hold a small ball of sushi rice in your right hand. Squeeze gently into a rectangular shape, like you did for nigiri. Place on a work surface. Attach one end of the nori to the middle of the rice ball.

2. Keep wrapping the nori around, making sure to keep it equidistant from the bottom. Mix chopped yellowjack fillet and scallion, and gently place on top of gunkanmaki. Garnish plate with wasabi and ginger.

Kani & Ebikko Gunkanmaki

SHRIMP ROE & CRAB SALAD

INGREDIENTS FOR 1 PORTION:

1 slightly rounded tablespoon sushi rice

1 gunkan nori band (⅛ sheet=7" x 1")

1½ teaspoons Kani & Ebikko Salad (recipe follows)

For the Kani & Ebikko Salad:

⅓ cup Kanikama flaked crab or imitation crab (surimi)

1 tablespoon shrimp roe

1 tablespoon minced chives

1 tablespoon Japanese or regular mayonnaise

1. Prepare the ingredients for the Kani & Ebikko Salad.

2. Mix all the ingredients together for the salad.

3. Moisten hands with water-vinegar mixture. Hold a small ball of sushi rice in your right hand. Squeeze gently into a rectangular shape and place on a work surface. Attach one end of the nori to the middle of the rice ball.

4. Keep wrapping the nori around, making sure to keep it equidistant from the bottom. Place the Kani & Ebikko Salad on top of the gunkanmaki and garnish plate with wasabi and ginger.

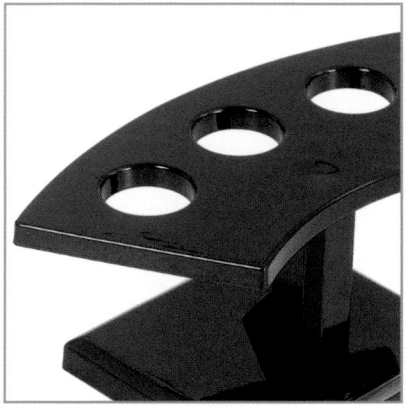

TEMAKI

Temaki means "hand roll" in Japanese, and in Japan, this is a popular sushi to make at home. That's because it loses its texture very quickly, so the best kind is made and served as fast as possible (not like in some restaurants)!

Unatama Temaki

BOILED EEL, TAMAGO, & SEASONED SHITAKE MUSHROOM

Seasoned Shitake Mushrooms

As you read in The Japanese Pantry (see p. 19), shitake mushrooms are very healthy (in addition to being delicious). In Japan, we use dried shitakes for flavoring soup and all kinds of other dishes, especially in the Zen kitchen, where they are slow-cooked in soy sauce and mirin and used as a meat substitute. They have a stronger aroma than fresh shitakes. When buying dried shitakes, always choose thick meaty-looking ones.

We also use fresh shitakes of course, especially for salads, tempura and grilling and sautéing with salt and pepper.

INGREDIENTS FOR 1 PORTION:

3½ ounces dried shitake mushrooms

1 cup water

2 tablespoons sugar

2 tablespoons mirin

2 tablespoons sake

4 tablespoons soy sauce

Brush the shitakes to remove any dust and loose pieces. Place in a bowl with the water. Cover and let soak overnight.

Drain and place mushrooms in a small saucepan. Add water to just cover and bring to a boil.

Add sugar and sake and mirin. Cook until reduced by half.

Add soy sauce and continue cooking until sauce evaporates.

INGREDIENTS FOR 1 PORTION:

½ sheet nori (7" long x 4" wide)

4 tablespoons sushi rice

2 pieces (1" x 3" each) fillet Unagi Kabayaki (Teriyaki-Broiled Eel, see recipe p. 61)

1 piece tamago (Japanese omelette, see recipe p. 62), 1½" x 3"

2 thin sticks hothouse cucumber (with peel)

1 Seasoned Shitake mushroom, cut in half or into thin strips

This temaki blends broiled eel and tamago—the famous Japanese omelette—with fabulous seasoned shitake mushrooms. For instructions on how to make tamago, check out my recipe (see p. 62). Directions for Seasoned Shitake follow.

1. Moisten hands with water-vinegar mixture. Hold the sushi rice in your right hand. Place the nori in your left hand, and spread the rice on half the sheet (the side with your fingers). Place all the rest of the ingredients for the filling diagonally.

2. Use the fingers of your right hand to fold the bottom right-hand corner of the nori over the filling.

3. Fold the bottom left-hand corner and bring it up to the upper right hand corner.

4. Tighten the cone if necessary, and check to see that it can be placed in a temaki stand without falling apart.

5. Place in a temaki stand and garnish with wasabi and ginger.

Negi Maguro Temaki

SCALLION & TUNA

"Negi" means scallion in Japanese, and "maguro" is, of course, tuna. (In Japan, we love to eat most of our fish and seafood with scallions.)

INGREDIENTS FOR 1 PORTION:

½ sheet nori (7" long x 4" wide)

4 tablespoons sushi rice

5" x ½" tuna fillet

1 teaspoon chopped scallion

1. Moisten hands with water-vinegar mixture. Hold the sushi rice in your right hand. Place the nori in your left hand, and spread the rice on half the sheet (the side with your fingers). Place all the rest of the ingredients for the filling diagonally.

2. Here's a close-up of the ingredients for anyone unsure of the correct placement. Now, use the fingers of your right hand to fold the bottom right hand corner of the nori over the filling. Fold the bottom left hand corner and bring it up to the upper right hand corner. Tighten the cone if necessary and check to see that it can be placed in a temaki stand without falling apart.

3. Place in a temaki stand and garnish with wasabi and ginger.

New Age Temaki

The next three temakis are the result of a totally foreign invasion. All were invented in America (so was spicy sauce) but are popular today among young people in Japan. Although you'll never catch a Japanese gourmet eating one (at least not in public), you'll find them in most sushi bars in America and Europe.

California Temaki

SHRIMP, CRAB SALAD & ASPARAGUS

Make sure to use very young (slim) asparagus for this recipe, or cut off the bottoms of thicker asparagus, and peel the stem before you steam them.

INGREDIENTS FOR 1 PORTION:

½ sheet nori (7" long x 4" wide)

4 tablespoons sushi rice

1 boiled shrimp

1-2 steamed asparagus

1 teaspoon Kani & Ebikko Salad (see p. 73)

1. Moisten hands with water-vinegar mixture. Hold the sushi rice in your right hand. Place the nori in your left hand, and spread the rice on half the sheet (the side with your fingers). Place all the rest of the ingredients for the filling diagonally. Place the nori in your left hand, and spread the rice on the finger side of the sheet (half the sheet). Place all the rest of the ingredients for the filling diagonally.

2. Here's a closer look at the correct placement of ingredients on the rice. Use the fingers of your right hand to fold the bottom right hand corner of the nori over the filling. Fold the bottom left hand corner and bring it up to the upper right hand corner. Tighten the cone if necessary and check to see that it can be placed in a temaki stand without falling apart.

3. Place in a temaki stand and garnish with wasabi and ginger.

Hokkai Temaki

SALMON, AVOCADO & CUCUMBER

"Hokkai" means North Ocean in Japanese, and this temaki reflects our belief that the best fish comes from the cold waters of the north.

INGREDIENTS FOR 1 PORTION:

½ sheet nori (7" long x 4" wide)

4 tablespoons sushi rice

5" long x ½" wide salmon fillet

5" long x ½" wide stick sliced avocado (in one or two pieces)

5" long x ½" wide (hothouse) cucumber stick

1. Moisten hands with water-vinegar mixture. Hold the sushi rice in your right hand. Place the nori in your left hand, and spread the rice on half the sheet (the side with your fingers). Place all the rest of the ingredients for the filling diagonally.

2. Use the fingers of your right hand to fold the bottom right hand corner of the nori over the filling. Fold the bottom left hand corner and bring it up to the upper right hand corner. Tighten the cone if necessary and check to see that it can be placed in a temaki stand without falling apart.

3. Place in a temaki stand and garnish with wasabi and ginger.

Norwegian Temaki

SALMON, GRILLED SALMON & SALMON ROE

A triple salmon experience, starring raw salmon fillet, grilled salmon and salmon roe—this temaki is a true gourmet treat!

INGREDIENTS FOR 1 PORTION:

½ sheet nori (7" long x 4" wide)

4 tablespoons sushi rice

5" x ½" salmon fillet

1 teaspoon grilled flaked salmon

5" long x ½" wide stick sliced avocado (in one or two pieces)

½ teaspoon spicy sauce (see recipe p. 39)

⅓ teaspoon salmon roe

1. Moisten hands with water-vinegar mixture. Hold the sushi rice in your right hand. Place the nori in your left hand, and spread the rice on half the sheet (the side with your fingers).

2. Place your thumbs under the bottom of the sushi mat, and use the remaining fingers to hold the filling in place.

3. Fold the bottom left hand corner and bring it up to the upper right hand corner. Tighten the cone if necessary and check to see that it can be placed in a temaki stand without falling apart.

4. Place in a temaki stand and garnish with wasabi and ginger. What a beautiful sight!

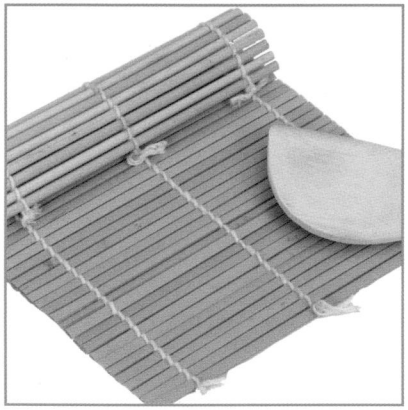

HOSOMAKI

Hosomaki is a "thin roll" filled with one or two kinds of ingredients. Although it looks simple, it's somewhat more difficult to make because the ingredients have to look good and fit together snugly, and the roll needs to be neatly done. Follow the instructions and pictures carefully, and I bet you'll get it on the first try!

Tekka Maki

TUNA

Tekka means "metal fire", probably the reason this sushi is so popular among the macho crowd in Tokyo!

INGREDIENTS FOR 1 ROLL (6 PIECES):

½ sheet nori (7" long x 4" wide)

6 tablespoons sushi rice

7" long x ½" wide tuna fillet

1. Place the nori on a sushi mat. Moisten hands with water-vinegar mixture and flatten the rice on top, leaving ½" from the bottom and sides. Place the tuna fillet in the middle of the rice.

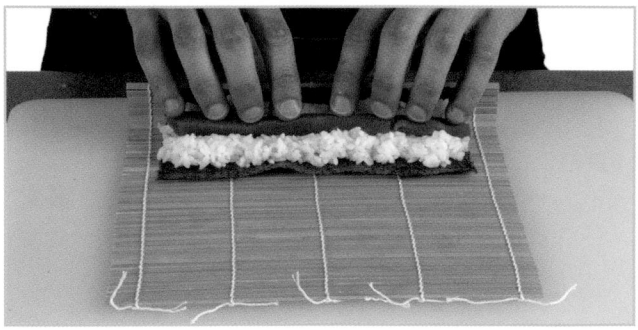

2. Place your thumbs under the bottom of the sushi mat and use your remaining fingers to hold the filling in place.

3. Bring the mat up to cover the filling, leaving 1" from the top edge of the nori, and enclose the roll.

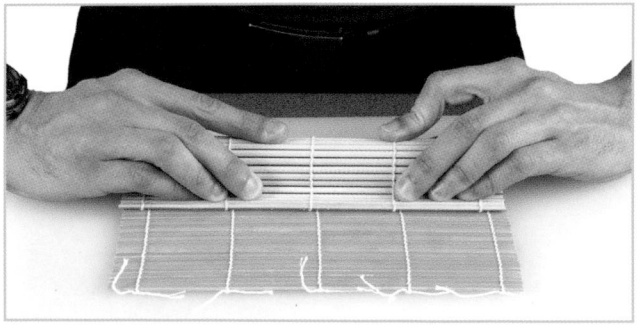

4. Press firmly with your fingers to tighten the roll, then raise the cover and bring forward slightly. Now close again over the entire roll firmly and remove the cover. (This seals the edge.)

5. This is how the roll should look. Does yours look this way? Slice the roll in half, and then each half into 3 pieces. Arrange on a serving platter with wasabi and ginger.

Ebikyu Maki

SHRIMP & CUCUMBER

This hosomaki is a special favorite among my friends, who enjoy the crisp taste of the cucumber ("Kyu" comes from Kyuri, which means cucumber), together with the simple but succulent taste of boiled shrimp (ebi).

INGREDIENTS FOR 1 ROLL (6 PIECES):

½ sheet nori (7" long x 4" wide)

6 tablespoons sushi rice

2 boiled shrimp

7½" hothouse cucumber stick (in 1 or 2 pieces)

¼ teaspoon sesame seeds, toasted in a dry frying pan

1. Place the nori on a sushi mat. Moisten hands with water-vinegar mixture and flatten the rice on top, leaving ½" from the bottom and sides. Place the boiled shrimp and cucumber in the middle of the rice. Sprinkle the sesame seeds on top.

2. Place your thumbs under the bottom of the sushi mat, and use your remaining fingers to hold the filling in place. Bring the mat up to cover the filling, leaving 1" from the top edge of the nori, and enclose the roll. Press firmly with your fingers to tighten the roll, then raise the cover and bring forward slightly. Now close again over the entire roll firmly and remove the cover. (This seals the edge.)

3. Slice the roll in half, and then each half into 3 pieces. Arrange on a serving platter with wasabi and ginger.

Unakyu Maki

EEL & CUCUMBER

INGREDIENTS FOR 1 ROLL (6 PIECES):

½ sheet nori (7" long x 4" wide)

6 tablespoons sushi rice

1½" x 7" fillet Unagi Kabayaki (Teriyaki-Broiled Eel, see recipe p. 61)

7½" hothouse cucumber stick (in 1 or 2 pieces)

¼ teaspoon sesame seeds, toasted in a dry frying pan

1. Place the nori on a sushi mat. Moisten hands with water-vinegar mixture and flatten the rice on top, leaving ½" from the bottom and sides. Place the eel and cucumber in the middle of the rice. Now place your thumbs under the bottom of the sushi mat, and use your remaining fingers to hold the filling in place.

2. Bring the mat up to cover the filling, leaving 1" from the top edge of the nori, and enclose the roll. Press firmly with your fingers to tighten the roll, then raise the cover and bring forward slightly. Now close again over the entire roll firmly and remove the cover. (This seals the edge.) Slice the roll in half. Then slice each half into 3 pieces. Arrange on a serving platter with wasabi and ginger.

Sake Maki

SALMON

INGREDIENTS FOR 1 ROLL (6 PIECES):

½ sheet nori (7" long x 4" wide)

6 tablespoons sushi rice

7" long x ½" wide salmon fillet

1. Place the nori on a sushi mat. Moisten hands with water-vinegar mixture and flatten the rice on top, leaving ½" from the bottom and sides. Place the fillet salmon in the middle of the rice. Now place your thumbs under the bottom of the sushi mat, and use your remaining fingers to hold the filling in place.

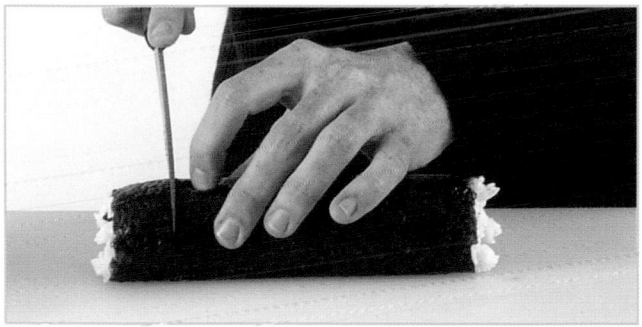

2. Bring the mat up to cover the filling, leaving 1" from the top edge of the nori, and enclose the roll. Press firmly with your fingers to tighten the roll, then raise the cover and bring forward slightly. Now close again over the entire roll firmly and remove the cover. (This seals the edge.) Slice the roll in half, and then each half into 3 pieces. Arrange on a serving platter with wasabi and ginger.

Hokkai Maki

SALMON & AVOCADO

INGREDIENTS FOR 1 ROLL (6 PIECES):

½ sheet nori (7" long x 4" wide)

6 tablespoons sushi rice

7" long x ¼" wide salmon fillet

7½" avocado stick (in 1 or 2 pieces)

1. Place the nori on a sushi mat. Moisten hands with water-vinegar mixture and flatten the rice on top, leaving ½" from the bottom and sides. Place the salmon and avocado in the middle of the rice.

2. Now place your thumbs under the bottom of the sushi mat, and use your remaining fingers to hold the filling in place.

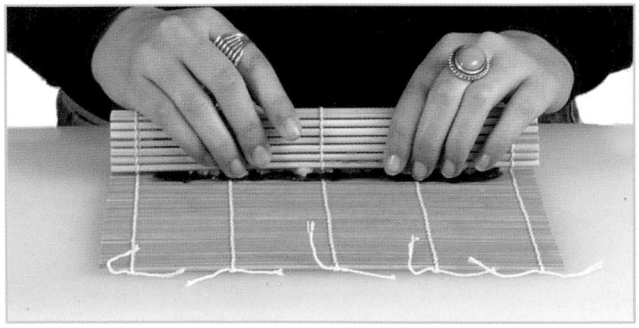

3. Bring the mat up to cover the filling, leaving 1" from the top edge of the nori, and enclose the roll. Press firmly with your fingers to tighten the roll, then raise the cover and bring forward slightly.

4. Now close again over the entire roll firmly and remove the cover. (This seals the edge.) Slice the roll in half, and then each half into 3 pieces. Arrange on a serving platter with wasabi and ginger.

Tamago Maki

JAPANESE OMELETTE

INGREDIENTS FOR 1 ROLL (6 PIECES):

½ sheet nori (7" long x 4" wide)

6 tablespoons sushi rice

7" long x ½" wide slice Tamago

Pinch of sesame seeds, toasted in a dry frying pan

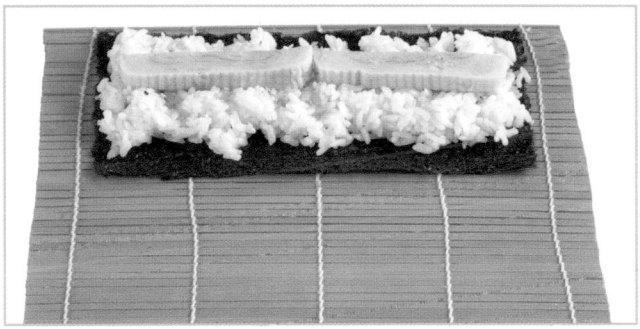

1. Place the nori on a sushi mat. Moisten hands with water-vinegar mixture and flatten the rice on top, leaving ½" from the bottom and sides. Place the Tamago in the middle of the rice. Sprinkle over the toasted sesame seeds. Now place your thumbs under the bottom of the sushi mat, and use the remaining fingers to hold the filling in place.

2. Bring the mat up to cover the filling, leaving 1" from the top edge of the nori, and enclose the roll. Press firmly with your fingers to tighten the roll, then raise the cover and bring forward slightly. Now close again over the entire roll firmly and remove the cover. (This seals the edge.) Slice the roll in half, and then each half into 3 pieces. Arrange on a serving platter with wasabi and ginger.

SAIMAKI

Inside-out rolls (Saimaki)—made with the rice placed first on the sushi mat and the ingredients arranged on top of the nori—are very popular around the world, but haven't really caught on in sushi bars in Japan. Although they look very complicated to make, they're really very easy if you follow the directions. Remember— -the order of placing the ingredients on the nori always depends on their texture: things that are sticky (like mayonnaise) are put on first, and only then the fish and other ingredients—that way you don't end up making a gooey mess out of it all!

Magurotaku Saimaki

TUNA & PICKLED RADISH

INGREDIENTS FOR 1 ROLL (6 PIECES):

½ sheet nori (7" long x 4" wide)

8 tablespoons sushi rice

7" long x ½" wide tuna fillet

7" long x ½" wide stick Takuwan (pickled daikon radish)

7½" hothouse cucumber stick (in 1 or 2 pieces)

3 tablespoons toasted black sesame seeds

1. Cover makisu (sushi bamboo mat) on both sides with plastic wrap. Moisten hands with water-vinegar mixture and cover the top of the mat with a layer of flattened sushi rice (it should be the same size or slightly larger than the nori we'll put on next). Place nori on the sushi rice. Arrange all the ingredients in the middle of the nori. Check to see if your ingredients are lined up like they are in this picture.

2. Now place your thumbs under the bottom of the sushi mat, and use your remaining fingers to hold the filling in place. Bring the mat up to cover the filling, leaving 1" from the top edge of the nori, and enclose the roll. Press firmly with your fingers to tighten the roll, then raise the cover and bring forward slightly. Now close again over the entire roll firmly and remove the cover. (This seals the edge.)

3. Sprinkle the black sesame seeds in a flat dish or platter and gently roll the saimaki in the seeds.

4. Slice the roll in half, and then each half into 3 pieces. Arrange on a serving platter with wasabi and ginger.

California Saimaki

SHRIMP, ASPARAGUS & CUCUMBER

INGREDIENTS FOR 1 ROLL (6 PIECES):

½ sheet nori (7" long x 4" wide)

8 tablespoons sushi rice

3 boiled shrimp

7½" hothouse cucumber stick (in 1 or 2 pieces)

7½" steamed asparagus (in 1 or 2 pieces)

2 tablespoons Kani & Ebikko Salad (see recipe p. 73)

1 tablespoon shrimp roe

1. Cover makisu (sushi bamboo mat) on both sides with plastic wrap. Moisten hands with water-vinegar mixture and cover the top of the mat with a layer of flattened sushi rice (it should be the same size or slightly larger than the nori we'll put on next).

2. Arrange all the ingredients in the middle of the nori.

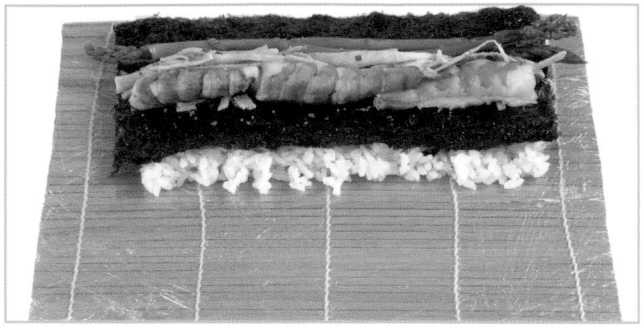

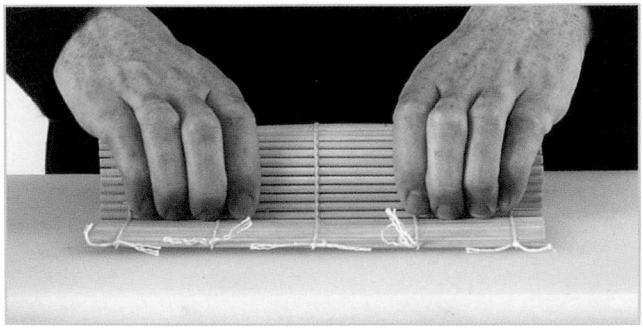

3. This is how to line up the ingredients. Now place your thumbs under the bottom of the sushi mat, and use the remaining fingers to hold the filling in place. Bring the mat up to cover the filling, leaving 1" from the top edge of the nori, and enclose the roll.

4. Press firmly with your fingers to tighten the roll, then raise the cover and bring forward slightly. Now close again over the entire roll firmly and remove the cover. (This seals the edge.) Slice the roll in half, and then each half into 3 pieces. Place shrimp roe in a flat dish. Pick up each piece individually and dip into the shrimp roe.

5. Arrange on a serving platter with wasabi and ginger.

Norwegian Saimaki

SALMON, AVOCADO & SCALLION

Having someone special over for dinner tonight? You're sure to impress him/her with this—a rich combination of sushi rice, two kinds of salmon, avocado and scallions on the inside, artfully wrapped with salmon fillet wrapper on the outside. Some people even call it a salmon lover's dream!

It starts like a regular saimaki roll, but the plastic wrap and sushi mat are replaced with a thin slice of salmon fillet, which is squeezed gently around the roll.

INGREDIENTS FOR 1 ROLL (6 PIECES):

½ sheet nori (7" long x 4" wide)

8 tablespoons sushi rice

Ruby lettuce

2 teaspoons Japanese or regular mayonnaise

½ teaspoon minced scallion

2 tablespoons grilled flaked salmon

7" long x ½" wide salmon fillet (for the filling)

7" long x ½" wide avocado stick (in 1 or 2 pieces)

7" long x 4-5" wide thin sliced (⅛") salmon fillet (for the wrapping)

1. Cover makisu (sushi bamboo mat) on both sides with plastic wrap. Moisten hands with water-vinegar mixture and cover the top of the mat with a layer of flattened sushi rice (it should be the same size or slightly larger than the nori we'll put on next) on top. Place nori on a sushi rice. Place a leaf or two of lettuce in the center of the rice, and using a plastic squeeze bottle filled with mayonnaise, make a horizontal line of mayo in the middle. Sprinkle on the scallions, and arrange the flaked salmon, salmon fillet and avocado stick on top.

2. Now place your thumbs under the bottom of the sushi mat, and use your remaining fingers to hold the filling in place. Bring the mat up to cover the filling, leaving 1" from the top edge of the nori, and enclose the roll. Press firmly with your fingers to tighten the roll, then raise the cover and bring forward slightly. Now close again over the entire roll firmly and remove the cover. (This seals the edge.)

3. Transfer the saimaki roll to a clean cutting board and cover the top with the remaining salmon fillet. Place a clean piece of plastic wrap on top, and cover with the makisu. Gently squeeze to attach the fillet to the top and sides of the roll. (It will cover three-quarters of the roll. It doesn't have to cover the underside.)

4. Remove plastic wrap from the saimaki and slice the roll in half.

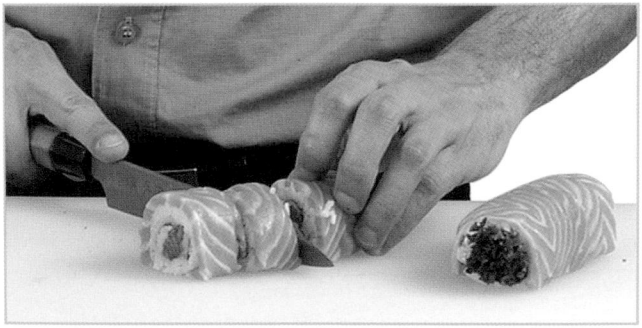

5. Slice each half into 3 pieces. Arrange on a serving platter with wasabi and ginger.

Futomaki (Traditional Thick Roll)

SHRIMP & BROILED EEL

Although this isn't an inside-out roll, I've added the recipe to this chapter because like saimaki, it is a thick roll with many ingredients. In Japan we use sea conger—sea eel—for making futomaki, but since it's more difficult to find, I suggest using unagi—fresh water eel—instead.

INGREDIENTS FOR 1 ROLL (6 PIECES):

1 sheet nori

12-14 tablespoons sushi rice (a little more than ¾ cup)

7" long x 1" wide Unagi Kabayaki (Teriyaki-Broiled Eel, see recipe p. 61)

3 boiled shrimp

7" long x 1" wide Tamago (see recipe p. 62)

2 seasoned shitake mushrooms, cut in half or into thin strips (see recipe p. 76)

2 tablespoons steamed spinach

1 teaspoon sakura denbu (sweet cod fish flakes)

½ teaspoon sesame seeds, toasted in a dry frying pan

1. Place the nori on a sushi mat. Moisten hands with water-vinegar mixture and flatten the rice on top, leaving 1" from the bottom and sides. This is how to line up the ingredients.

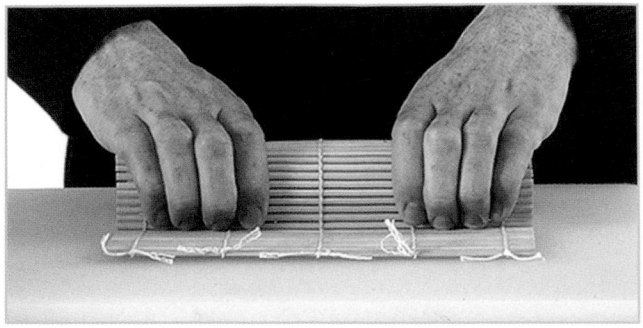

2. Now place your thumbs under the bottom of the sushi mat, and use your remaining fingers to hold the filling in place. Bring the mat up to cover the filling, leaving 1" from the top edge of the nori, and enclose the roll. Press firmly with your fingers to tighten the roll, then raise the cover and bring forward slightly. Now close again over the entire roll firmly and remove the cover. (This seals the edge.)

3. Slice the roll into 6 pieces. (Or better yet, slice the roll in half, and each half into 3 pieces.) Arrange on a serving platter with wasabi and ginger.

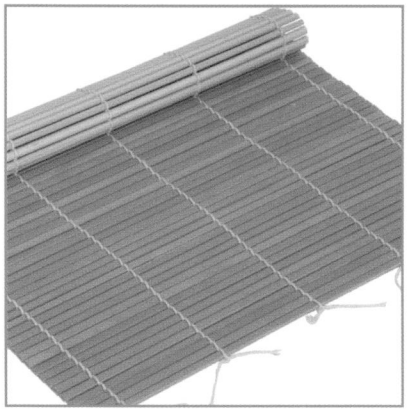

ALL-VEGETARIAN SUSHI

These days, there are many sushi lovers who prefer to eat vegetarian food, or order vegetarian sushi as part of their selection. Whether for health or humane reasons, or just to add a pleasing crunch, veggie sushi provides a touch of color and aesthetic harmony to any sushi selection.

Shitake Maki

SHITAKE MUSHROOMS

INGREDIENTS FOR 1 ROLL (6 PIECES):

½ sheet nori (7" long x 4" wide)

6 tablespoons sushi rice

1 seasoned shitake mushroom, cut in half or into thin strips (see recipe p. 76)

Pinch of toasted sesame seeds

1. Place the nori on a sushi mat. Moisten hands with water-vinegar mixture and flatten the rice on top, leaving 1" from the bottom and sides. Place the shitake mushroom in the middle of the rice. Sprinkle over the toasted sesame seeds. This is how to line up the ingredients. Now place your thumbs under the bottom of the sushi mat, and use your remaining fingers to hold the filling in place.

2. Bring the mat up to cover the filling, leaving 1" from the top edge of the nori, and enclose the roll. Press firmly with your fingers to tighten the roll, then raise the cover and bring forward slightly. Now close again over the entire roll firmly and remove the cover. (This seals the edge.) Slice the roll in half, and then each half into 3 pieces. Arrange on a serving platter with wasabi and ginger.

Oshinko Maki

PICKLED RADISH

Most people think that "Oshinko" means pickled daikon, but the word really refers to all kinds of pickles, which we Japanese love to prepare at home.

INGREDIENTS FOR 1 ROLL (6 PIECES):

½ sheet nori (7" long x 4" wide)

6 tablespoons sushi rice

7" long ½" wide Takuwan (pickled radish)

Pinch toasted sesame seeds

1. Place the nori on a sushi mat. Moisten hands with water-vinegar mixture and flatten the rice on top, leaving ½" from the bottom and sides. Place the Takuwan in the middle of the rice. Sprinkle on the toasted sesame seeds. Now place your thumbs under the bottom of the sushi mat, and use your remaining fingers to hold the filling in place.

2. Bring the mat up to cover the filling, leaving 1" from the top edge of the nori, and enclose the roll. Press firmly with your fingers to tighten the roll, then raise the cover and bring forward slightly. Now close again over the entire roll firmly and remove the cover. (This seals the edge.) Slice the roll in half, and then each half into 3 pieces. Arrange on a serving platter with wasabi and ginger.

Saishoku Saimaki

MIXED VEGETABLES

Saishoku means vegetarian in Japanese, and this saimaki is an especially healthy feast for vegetarians and non-vegetarians alike. In addition to contrasting textures (like avocado and carrot), it contains so many vitamins and minerals that's hard to count.

Like the Norwegian saimaki, this roll has a "wrapper" around it—made of avocado instead of salmon—which gives it a delightful taste and unique "look".

Don't feel you have to make the recipe exactly as written—feel free to experiment with other vegetables and/or with regular or seasoned tofu.

INGREDIENTS FOR 1 ROLL (6 PIECES):

½ sheet nori (7" long x 3½" wide)

8 tablespoons sushi rice

7" long x ½" wide piece Takuwan

7" long x ½" wide avocado stick (in 1 or 2 pieces)

1 tablespoon steamed leaf spinach, well drained

7" long hothouse cucumber stick

7" long carrot stick

1-2 seasoned shitake mushrooms, cut in half (see recipe p. 76)

Pinch toasted sesame seeds

For the wrapping:

Enough 5" long x ⅛" thick avocado slices to cover the roll

1. Cover makisu (sushi bamboo mat) with plastic wrap. Moisten hands with water-vinegar mixture and flatten the sushi rice on top (it should be the same size as the piece of nori).

2. Place nori over the sushi rice, and lay all the ingredients in the middle of the nori, like you see in this picture. Now place your thumbs under the bottom of the sushi mat, and use the remaining fingers to hold the filling in place.

3. Bring the mat up to cover the filling, leaving 1" from the top edge of the nori, and enclose the roll. Press firmly with the fingers to tighten, then raise the cover and bring forward slightly. Now close again over the entire roll firmly and remove the cover. (This seals the edge.) Place the Saimaki on a cutting board. Drape the thin avocado slices over the roll. (It should cover all but the bottom of the roll).

4. Gently cover the roll with the avocado slices to replace the bamboo mat. Press the roll gently but firmly to help the avocado adhere to the rice. Remove the mat and plastic wrap from the Saimaki. Slice the roll in half, and each half into 3 pieces. Arrange on a serving platter with wasabi and ginger.

Aspara Maki

ASPARAGUS

Although asparagus aren't native to Japan, they've been lovingly adopted by the Japanese. We still haven't given them a Japanese name however!

INGREDIENTS FOR 1 ROLL (6 PIECES):

½ sheet nori (7" long x 4" wide)

6 tablespoons sushi rice

7" long steamed this asparagus spears or 1 thick one (peeled)

Pinch of toasted sesame seeds

1. Place the nori on a sushi mat. Moisten hands with water-vinegar mixture and flatten the rice on top, leaving ½" from the bottom and sides.

2. Place the asparagus in the middle of the rice. Add roasted sesame seeds. Now place your thumbs under the bottom of the sushi mat and use your remaining fingers to hold the filling in place.

3. From the top edge of the nori, enclose the roll. Press firmly with your fingers to tighten the roll, then raise the cover and bring forward slightly. Now close again over the entire roll firmly and remove the cover. (This seals the edge.) Slice the roll in half, and then each half into 3 pieces.

4. Arrange on a serving platter with wasabi and ginger.

Kappa Maki

CUCUMBER

Place the nori on a sushi mat. Moisten hands with water-vinegar mixture and flatten the rice on top, leaving 1" from the bottom and sides. Place the cucumber sticks in the middle of the rice, and sprinkle over the toasted sesame seeds. Now place your thumbs under the bottom of the sushi mat, and use your remaining fingers to hold the filling in place. Bring the mat up to cover the filling, leaving 1" from the top edge of the nori, and enclose the roll. Press firmly with your fingers to tighten the roll, then raise the cover and bring forward slightly. Now close again over the entire roll firmly and remove the cover. Slice the roll in half, and then each half into 3 pieces. Arrange on a serving platter with wasabi and ginger.

INGREDIENTS FOR 1 ROLL (6 PIECES):

½ sheet nori (7½" long x 4" wide)

6 tablespoons sushi rice

7" long (hothouse) cucumber sticks

Pinch of toasted sesame seeds

JAPANESE SOUPS

Misoshiru

MISO SOUP

The first time I walked into a sushi bar in New York, I was really surprised to see everyone sipping the same kind of miso soup with little tofu cubes and wakame in it. In fact, every Japanese restaurant that I visited in America seemed to serve the same kind of soup. Why was I surprised? Because in Japan, this is never done. While miso soup may be an integral part of a sushi meal, it is always served with fish or seafood. The kind served in America—with tofu and seaweed—traditionally usually goes with other types of meals.

Miso soup is like an espresso coffee—it's not the kind of soup which improves with taste the longer it is heated; it just becomes very salty. (In fact, boiling miso soup destroys the beneficial enzymes it contains.) So it's better to make or heat the amount you want just before serving.

If you use dashi no moto (instant fish soup powder), check the flavor before you buy; it comes in various flavors like pure bonito, pure sardine or mixed bonito and sardine. For serving with sushi, you'll want to have pure bonito because of its mild flavor. For serving with teriyaki or other Japanese meals, sardine or mixed sardine-bonito is fine.

INGREDIENTS FOR 6 SERVINGS:
(depending on size of soup cup)

4 cups water

One 1" x 4" piece dried kombu seaweed

½ cup Kezuribushi (bonito flakes) or 1 tablespoon dashi no moto

4 tablespoons Aka miso

2 tablespoons sake

1. In a saucepan, bring water to a boil over medium heat. Place kombu in the water and remove after 10 seconds. Add bonito flakes or dashi no moto.

2. Let stand 15 seconds, then strain through a wire-mesh strainer. If using dashi no moto, it is unnecessary to strain the soup. At this point you can add other ingredients like the head of the shrimp (from making butterflied shrimp), fresh fillet of fish or other seafood or vegetables that have been lightly boiled. Cook for 2-3 minutes over medium heat (cooking time depends on type of ingredients). Remove from heat.

3. Pass the miso through the strainer into the soup, and stir to blend.

4. Mmm. Doesn't this look good! It's miso soup with a shrimp head and scallion garnish.

More Miso Soup Possibilities...

All ingredients that need to be boiled should be prepared before starting Step 2 at left. Fresh ingredients should be added during Step 2.

1. Lightly steamed or boiled fish fillet (or leftover head and bones)
2. Fresh whole shrimp
3. Fresh flaked crab
4. Lightly boiled chicken, cut into bite-sized pieces.
5. Cooked pork, sliced very thin
6. Cooked duck, sliced very thin
7. Poached egg—add an already-poached egg just before serving. (Lightly boiled or steamed thinly sliced potato, onion, carrot or asparagus go well together with the egg)
8. Tofu cut into small cubes
9. Wakame seaweed (fresh or reconstituted)
10. Nameko mushroom
11. Fresh or grilled wild mushrooms cut into bite-sized pieces
12. Boiled potato, peeled and sliced to size you want before boiling
13. Boiled sweet potato, peeled and sliced to size you want before boiling
14. Fresh onion, sliced
15. Fresh bean sprouts
16. Fresh carrot, sliced as desired
17. Fresh spinach (Japanese spinach should be boiled before adding)
18. Fresh eggplant cut to size as desired (fried eggplant is also great!)
19. Fresh snow peas, tips removed
20. Fresh asparagus spears, cut to include tips and tender part of stem only

Garnishes:

1. Green onions (scallions), minced
2. Chili powder

Suimono

FISH-FLAVORED CLEAR SOUP

It's suimono, not miso, that's actually the ultimate soup to serve with sushi. Unlike miso soup, which is an everyday soup for us, suimono has a noble image for the Japanese. Suimono does not taste good after it has been cooked for a long time over a hot stove. Don't worry, though. It's so easy and quick to prepare that you'll understand why we make or heat each portion just before serving.

If you use dashi no moto (instant fish soup powder), it's best to check the flavor before buying. Sardine flavor is not suitable for suimono. This delicate soup may also be made with any fresh fish you have on hand, instead of soup powder and bonito flakes seasonings. (See my list of variations on the next page.)

INGREDIENTS FOR 6-8 SERVINGS:
(depending on size of soup cup)

4 cups mineral water

½ cup sake

One 1" x 4" piece dried kombu seaweed

½ cup Kezuribushi (bonito flakes) or 1 tablespoon dashi no moto

2 teaspoons sea salt

A few drops of soy sauce

1 medium carrot, sliced and steamed or boiled

⅓ cup fresh spinach, stems removed, steamed or boiled

¼ cup daikon strips, lightly steamed or boiled

1. Place the water and sake in a medium saucepan. Bring to a boil and add the kombu. Remove with chopsticks after 10 seconds.

2. Add the bonito and strain out after 15 seconds. (Or add the dashi no moto.)

3. Add the sea salt. Add a few drops of soy sauce.

4. Add the boiled or steamed carrots, spinach and radish.

5. Here's how it looks when it's done.

More Suimono Soup Possibilities...

All ingredients that need to be boiled should be prepared before starting Step 2 on the previous page. Fresh ingredients should be added during Step 2.

1. Light boiled fish fillet (or leftover head and bones).
2. Grilled fish fillet—flaked.
3. Boiled peeled shrimp—boiled in dashi soup and peeled
4. Kamaboko (ready-made fish dumpling) sliced ⅛" thick
5. Boiled chicken cut into bite-sized pieces
6. Lightly boiled chicken "meatball"—minced chicken with ginger and salt
7. Poached egg—add to the finished soup. Goes well with steamed carrot, spinach, asparagus etc., or fresh snow peas
8. Tofu, cubed
9. Wakame seaweed, fresh or reconstituted
10. Fresh or grilled wild mushroom, cut into bite-sized pieces
11. Fresh radishes, sliced as desired
12. Fresh carrots, sliced as desired
13. Fresh spinach (if using Japanese spinach, boil before using)
14. Fresh snow peas
15. Fresh green onions cut to 1½"-2½" long
16. Fresh asparagus tips (with tender part of stem only)

Garnishes for ready portion of Suimono:

Fresh green onion (scallions), minced

A few drops of yuzu orange or lime juice

Kawarizushi

In this last chapter of the book, I'm feeling a little nostalgic, so I decided to close with these very special sushi, the kind you'll never find in sushi bars. These are the sushi that you'd probably find a Japanese mother or grandmother busy making, out of all kinds of leftovers she has at home. The techniques are fun and the ingredients are flexible, so feel free to experiment, and explore your own creativity! I give examples of a few variations with each one, just for starters.

Ohinasama Chirashi

SALMON & BOILED EEL

"Chirashi" is simply sushi rice with a topping, served in a sushi oke (traditional sushi pot). "Ohinasama Hinamatsuri" means Girls' Day, and although this is not exactly the traditional sushi served on that holiday in Japan (a traditional one might be decorated with a cherry blossom that begins to appear at the same time in March), it's the one my daughter likes best!

INGREDIENTS:

2 cups sushi rice

1 tablespoon toasted sesame seeds, toasted in a dry frying pan

½ tablespoon chopped pickled ginger

1 rounded tablespoon flaked grilled salmon

1 rounded tablespoon chopped Unagi Kabayaki (see recipe p. 61)

1 teaspoon sakura denbu (sweet cod powder)

½ seasoned shitake mushroom (see recipe p. 76) sliced thin (⅛")

1 asparagus tip, steamed or boiled and sliced 1½" long

1 teaspoon cooked sweet corn

1. Place the ingredients on a work surface.

2. Add the sesame seeds and ginger to the rice.

3. Use your fingers to mix the ingredients together.

4. Transfer the rice mixture to a sushi-oke or flat-bottomed ceramic bowl.

5. Add remaining ingredients and mix lightly.

Youfuu Oshizushi (Western-Style Pressed Sushi)

SALMON

Youfuu means "western," since as I mentioned before, salmon is not typically used for sushi or sashimi in Japan (although we do like it grilled or fried). This one is made with an oshizushi press, easily available at Japanese or Asian markets.

INGREDIENTS FOR 6 PIECES, SERVES 2:

6 slices salmon fillet (½ ounce, 2" long, 1½" wide, ⅛" thick)

6-8 tablespoons sushi rice

2 lemons, cut in half and sliced

Fresh dill sprigs for garnish

1. Dip entire frame of press in water and lightly dry with a paper towel. Remove the cover and place the salmon fillets inside, with edges overlapping.

2. Place the rice over the salmon in an even layer.

3. Replace the cover and press down lightly.

4. Use your thumbs to hold down the cover while you grasp the edges of the outer frame and remove it.

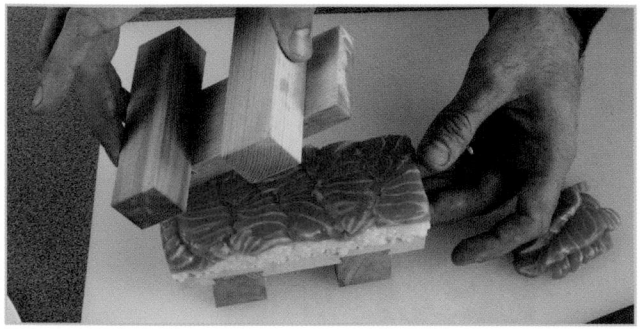

5. Turn over and remove the frame.

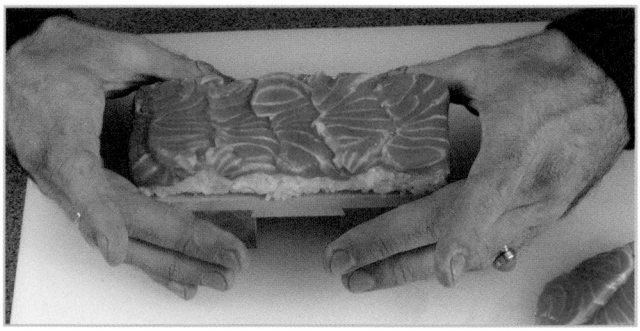

6. Slice the sushi in half and then slice each half into 3 pieces. Arrange on a serving platter with lemon slices in between. Garnish with dill. Serve with wasabi and ginger.

Sushi Cake

CHICKEN & CASHEW NUT TERIYAKI

My special sushi cake is made using something borrowed from western kitchens—a 2½" stainless steel pastry ring usually used for making perfectly round pancakes, eggs, or pastry. This recipe is great for everyone—especially those who prefer an alternative to fish—though you can use raw fish or any other topping if desired.

We make this sushi directly on the serving plate—since once it's there you won't want to disturb it!

INGREDIENTS FOR EACH SERVING:

1 butterhead lettuce leaf

6 tablespoons sushi rice

INGREDIENTS FOR CHICKEN CASHEW TERIYAKI:

1 tablespoon chicken thigh meat, cut into ¼" chunks

1 tablespoon chopped cashew nuts

2 tablespoons teriyaki sauce

Chives for garnish

Before you begin to make the sushi, you need to prepare the filling: Grease a small frying pan with a little corn oil and gently stir-fry the chicken. Add the cashew nuts and continue to stir-fry 30 seconds. Pour in the teriyaki sauce, and cook over medium-low heat until the chicken is glazed and the sauce is reduced by half. May be served warm or cold.

1. Place a whole lettuce leaf on a serving platter. Wash the ring in cold water and dry with a paper towel. Place over the leaf.

2. Fill the ring with half the rice, pressing down lightly.

3. Spoon a layer of the prepared filling over the rice.

4. Set another layer of rice on top.

5. Use your thumbs to hold down the rice, while gently removing the ring with your fingers.

6. Place another spoonful of the chicken mixture on top. Garnish with the chives and serve.

Temarizushi

TUNA, SALMON & AVOCADO

"Te" means hand and "Mari" means ball. The name actually derives from the Samurai era, when the daughters of the wealthy samurais were given beautifully colored and designed (hand) balls made of silk or other expensive materials, to play with. These are typical sushi that a Japanese mom would make at home—and kids (and friends) will love to make, too!

INGREDIENTS FOR 3 PIECES:

3 rice balls, each made with:

1½ tablespoons sushi rice

1½" x 1½" x ⅛" thick slice of tuna

1½" x 1½" x ⅛" thick slice of salmon

1½" x 1½" x ⅛" thick slice of avocado

Minced chives

Salmon roe

Toasted black sesame seeds

1 teaspoon teriyaki sauce

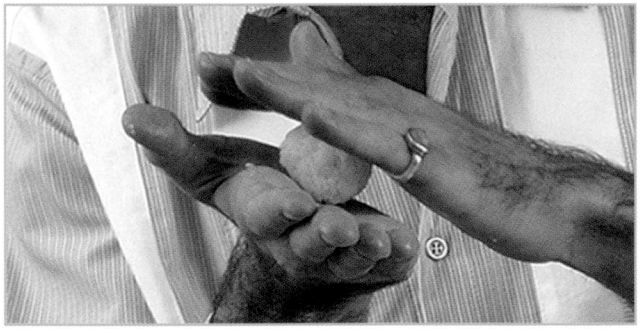

1. Moisten hands with water-vinegar mixture and form 3 rice balls.

2. Cut an 8" square of plastic wrap. Put one of the fillets in the middle. Place a rice ball on top of the fish fillet.

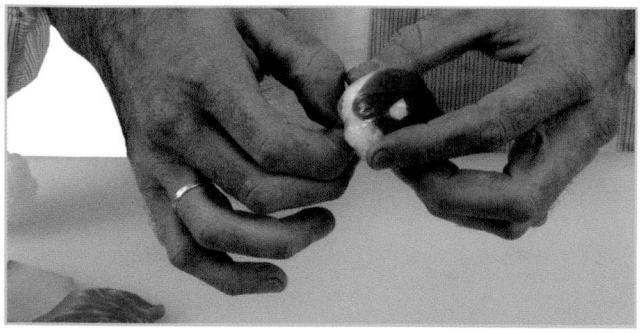

3. Bring up the corners of the plastic wrap to enclose the bundle.

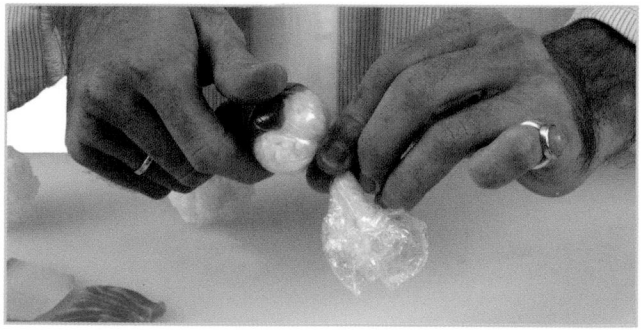

4. Twist the edges tightly. Repeat with the other fillets and remaining rice. Garnish the salmon with salmon roe, the tuna with minced chives, and the avocado with teriyaki sauce and black sesame seeds.

Saladamaki

JUMBO SHRIMP & LETTUCE

Japanese kids love mayonnaise (just like their American counterparts), so many a mother will use leftover jumbo shrimp, crab, fish dumplings grilled chicken, or even smoked meats, to make this sushi.

INGREDIENTS FOR 1 ROLL (6 PIECES):

1 sheet nori

10-12 tablespoons sushi rice

3 boiled shrimp

Butterhead lettuce leaves

1 tablespoon Japanese or regular mayonnaise

1. Place the nori on a sushi mat. Moisten hands with water-vinegar mixture and flatten the rice on top, leaving 1" from the bottom and sides.

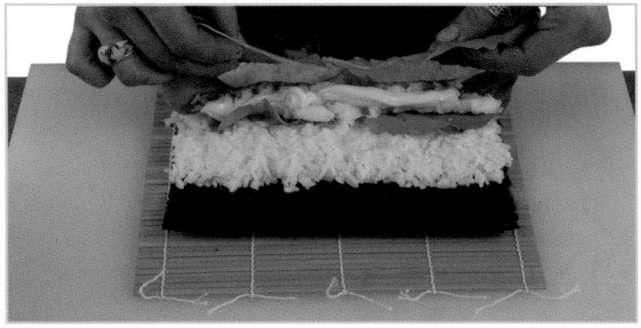

2. Cut the lettuce leaf in half and place on the rice. Put the shrimp and a squeeze of mayonnaise inside.

3. Close the lettuce over the filling.

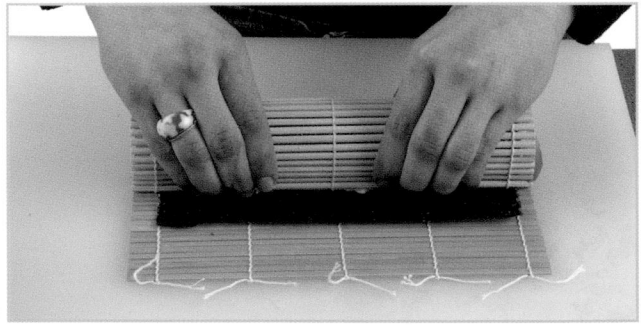

4. Now place your thumbs under the bottom of the sushi mat, and use your remaining fingers to hold the filling in place. Bring the mat up to cover the filling, leaving 1" from the top edge of the nori.

5. Enclose the roll and press firmly with your fingers to tighten. Raise the cover and bring forward slightly. Now close again over the entire roll firmly and remove the cover.

6. Slice the roll into 6 pieces. (Or slice the roll in half, and then each half into 3 pieces.) Arrange on a serving platter with wasabi and ginger.

Index

A
Abalone 30
Amberjack 30
Arkshell 30
Arranged Maguro Sashimi 46
Arranged Tamago Nigiri 63
Aspara Maki 106
Asparagus
  Aspara Maki 106
  California Saimaki 94
  California Temaki 79
  Misoshiru 110
  Ohinasama Chirashi 116
  Suimono 112
Avocado
  Hokkai Maki 88
  Hokkai Temaki 80
  Norwegian Saimaki 96
  Norwegian Temaki 81
  Saishoku Saimaki 105
  Spicy Shrimp Gunkanmaki 71
  Temarizushi 122

B
Bass 30
  Kawa Suzuki Arai 48
Bean Sprouts
  Misoshiru 111

C
California Saimaki 94
California Temaki 79
Carrots 22
  Misoshiru 110
  Saishoku Saimaki 105
  Sashimi Vegetables 44
  Suimono 112
Cashew Nuts
  Sushi Cake 120
Chicken 16
  Misoshiru 110
  Saladmaki 124
  Spicy Sauce 39
  Suimono 112
  Sushi Cake 120
Chili
  Misoshiru 110
  Spicy Sauce 39
Chives
  Kani & Ebikko Salad 73
  Sake Salmon 47
  Sushi Cake 120
  Temarizushi 122
Clam
  Cockle Clam 30
  Large Clam 29
  Surf Clam 30
Corn
  Dashimaki Tamago 62
  Ohinasama Chirashi 116
  Sushi Cake 120
Crab
  California Temaki 79
  Kani & Ebbiko Gunkanmaki 73
  Misoshiru 110
  Saladmaki 124
Cucumber 22
  California Saimaki 94
  Ebbiko Gunkanmaki 67
  Ebikyu Maki 85
  Hokkai Temaki 80
  Ikura Gunkanmaki 66
  Kappa Maki 107
  Maguro & Uzura Gunkanmaki 68
  Magurotaku Saimaki 92
  Saishoku Saimaki 104
  Sashimi Vegetables 44
  Takosumiso 49
  Unakyu Maki 86
  Unatama Temaki 76
Cuttlefish 29

D
Dashi No Moto 21
  Dashimaki Tamago 62
  Misoshiru 110
  Suimono 112
Dashimaki Tamago 62
Duck: Mishoshiru 111

E
Ebi Nigiri 58
Ebikko Gunkanmaki 67
Ebikyu Maki 85
Eel 15, 29
  Futomaki 98
  How to Prepare Unagi Kabayaki 61
  Ohinasama Chirashi 116
  Unagi Kabayaki Nigiri 60
  Unakyo Maki 86
  Unatama Temaki 76
Eggplant: Misoshiru 111
Eggs
  Dashimaki Tamago 62
  Maguro & Uzura Gunkanmaki 68
Poached Egg
  Mishoshiru 111
  Suimono 113
Quail Egg Maguro & Uzura Gunkanmaki 68
Tamago Nigiri 62

F
Fillet 16, 29, 30
  Choosing a fillet 31
  Grilled Tuna Salad Gunkanmaki 70
  Hokkai Maki 88
  Hokkai Temaki 80
  How to fillet a whole fish 31
  How to Slice a Fillet for Sashimi 43
  Kawa Suzuki Arai 48
  Maguro Nigiri 57
  Magurotaku Saimaki 92
  Misoshiro 111
  Negi Maguro Temaki 78
  Negi Shima-Aji Gunkanmaki 72
  Norwegian Saimaki 96
  Norwegian Temaki 81
  Sake Maki 87
  Spicy Tuna Gunkanmaki 69
  Suimono 113
  Tekka Maki 84
  Temarizushi 122
  How to Prepare Unagi Kabayaki 61
  Unagi Kabayaki Nigiri 60
  Unakyu Maki 86
  Unatama Temaki 76
  Youfuu Oshizushi 118
Flounder 30
Flying Fish Roe 30
Futomaki 98

G
Ginger 19, 21, 29
  How to Make Pickled Ginger 23
Green Tea 18, 19, 21

Takosumiso 49
Grilled Tuna Salad Gunkanmaki 70
Gunkanmaki 64-73

H
Halfbeak 29
Herring Roe 29
Hokkai Maki 88
Hokkai Temaki 80
Horse Mackerel 29
Hosomaki 82-89

I
Ikura Gunkanmaki 66
Inari 21

K
Kampyo 22
Kani & Ebikko Gunkanmaki 73
Kani & Ebikko Salad 73
California Saimaki 94
California Temaki 79
Karashisumiso Sauce 37
Kawa Suzuki Arai 48
Takosumiso 49
Kezuribushi 19
Dashimaki Tamago 62
Misoshiru 110
Suimono 112
Kitchen tools 14-16
Kombu 21
Dried 22
Misoshiru 110
Suimono 112
Sushizu 36
Tsukuri Jyouyu 37

L
Lemon
Sake Sashimi 47
Youfuu Oshizushi 118
Lettuce
Norwegian Saimaki 96
Saladmaki 124
Sashimi Vegetables 44
Sushi Cake 120
Lime Juice 29
Karashisumiso Sauce 37
Suimono 110

M
Maccha 21
Mackerel 29
Maguro Nigiri 57
Maguro & Uzaru Gunkanmaki 68
Magurotaku Saimaki 92
Mayonnaise 20
Grilled Tuna Salad Gunkanmaki 70
Kani & Ebikko Gunkanmaki 73
Norwegian Saimaki 96
Saladmaki 124
Spicy Sauce 39
Mirin 19, 21, 22
Seasoned Shitake Mushrooms 76
Teriyaki Sauce 38
Tsukuri Jyouyu 37
Miso 18, 22
Karashisumiso Sauce 37
Misoshiru 110
Suimono 112
Mushrooms 22
Futomaki 98
Mishoshiru 110
Saishoku Saimaki 104
Seasoned Shitake Mushrooms 76
Shitake Maki 102
Unatama Temaki 76

N
Negi Maguro Temaki 78
Negi Shima-Aji Gunkamaki 72
Nori 14, 19
Nigiri 54-63
Norwegian Saimaki 96
Norwegian Temaki 81

O
Octopus 29
Takosumiso 49
Ohinasama Chirashi 116
Onion
Grilled Tuna Salad Gunkanmaki 70
Misoshiru 111
Suimono 113
Oshinko
Arranged Maguro Sashimi 46
Oshinko Maki 103
Sake Sashimi 47
Sashimi Vegetables 44
Oshinko Maki 103

P
Pantry, the Japanese 19
Parsley
Sashimi Vegetables 44
Pickled Ginger 19, 21
How to Make Pickled Ginger 23
Ohinasama Chirashi 116
Pickled Radish
Magurotaku Saimaki 92
Oshinko Maki 103
Sashimi Vegetables 44
Plums 19
Pork
Misoshiru 111
Potato
Misoshiru 111

R
Raayu
Spicy Sauce 39
Radish 20, 22
Magurotaku Saimaku 92
Oshinko Maki 103
Sashimi Vegetables 44
Suimono 113
Red Snapper 30
Rice—see Sushi Rice

S
Saimaki 90-99
Saishoku Saimaki 105
Sake 18, 19, 21, 42, 56, 62
Arranged Maguro Sashimi 46
Dashimaki Tamago 62
How to Make Sushizu 36
Misoshiru 110
Sake Maki 87
Sake Sashimi 47
Suimono 112
Takosumiso 49
Teriyaki Sauce 38
Unatama Temaki 76
Sake Maki 87
Sake Sashimi 47
Sakura Denbu
Futomaki 98
Ohinasama Chirashi 116

Saladmaki 124
Salmon 15, 30, 31, 42
Arranged Maguro Sashimi 46
Hokkai Maki 88
Hokkai Temaki 80
Ikura Gunkanmaki 66
Maguro Nigiri 56
Norwegian Temaki 81
Norwegian Saimaki 96
Ohinasama Chirashi 116
Saishoku Saimaki 105
Sake Maki 87
Sake Sashimi 47
Temarizushi 122
Youfuu Oshizushi 118
Sardine 21, 28, 29
Misoshiru 110
Suimono 112
Sashimi 40-49
Sashimi Vegetables 44
Sauces 34-39
Scallop 30
Sea Bass 30
Sea Brim 30
Sea Urchin 30
Seasoned Shitake Mushrooms 76
Sesame 16, 20
Arranged Maguro Sashimi 44
Aspara Maki 106
Ebikyu Maki 85
Futomaki 98
Kappa Maki 107
Magurotaki Saimaki 92
Ohinasama Chirashi 116
Oshinko Maki 103
Saishoku Saimaki 104
Shitake Maki 102
Spicy Sauce 39
Tamago Maki 89
Temarizushi 122
Unakyu Maki 86
Shitake Maki 102
Shrimp 29, 30
California Saimaki 94
California Temaki 79
Ebi Nigiri 58
Ebikyu Maki 85
Futomaki 98
Hokkai Maki 88
How to Boil and Butterfly Jumbo Shrimp 59
Misoshiru 110
Saladmaki 124
Spicy Shrimp Gunkanmaki 71
Suimono 113
Shrimp Roe 30
California Saimaki 94
Ebikko Gunkanmaki 67
Kani & Ebikko Gunkanmaki 73
Soups 108-113
Soy 17, 19, 20, 22, 29
Real Wasabi 23
Spicy Sauce 39
Suimono 112
Takosumiso 49
Tamago Nigiri 62
Teriyaki Sauce 38
Tsukuri Jyouju 37
Unatama Temaki 76
Special Soy Sauce for Sashimi 37
Spicy Sauce 39
Norwegian Temaki 81
Spicy Shrimp Gunkanmaki 71
Spicy Tuna Gunkanmaki 69
Spicy Shrimp Gunkanmaki 71
Spicy Tuna Gunkanmaki 69
Spinach
Futomaki 98
Misoshiru 111
Saishoku Saimaki 104
Suimono 113
Suimono 112
Sushi Cake 120
Sushi Rice 50-53
Sushi Vinegar 36

T
Tableware 17-18
Takosumiso 49
Tamago Maki 89
Tamago Nigiri 62
Arranged Tamago Nigiri 63
Tekka Maki 84
Temaki 74-81
Temarizushi 122
Teriyaki 38
How to Prepare Unagi Kabayaki 61
Misoshiru 110
Sushi Cake 120
Temarizushi 122
Unagi Kabayaki Nigiri 60
Unatama Temaki 76
Tofu 21
Inari 21
Misoshiru 110
Saishoku Saimaki 104
Suimono 113
Tomato
Spicy Sauce 39
Tuna 29, 31, 42
Arranged Maguro Sashimi 46
How to Slice a Fillet for Sashimi 43
Hibachi 15
Grilled Tuna Salad Gunkanmaki 70
Maguro Nigiri 57
Maguro & Uzura Gunkanmaki 68
Magurotaku Saimaki 92
Negi Maguro Temaki 78
Spicy Tuna Gunkanmaki 69
Tekka Maki 84
Temarizushi 122

U
Unagi Kabayaki 61
Unagi Kabayaki Nigiri 60
Unakyu Maki 86
Unatama Temaki 76

V
Vinegar 15, 20, 21, 29, 42
How to boil and butterfly Jumbo Shrimp 59
How to Make Pickled Ginger 23
How to Make Sushizu 36
Sushi Rice 52
Takosumiso 49
Water-vinegar mixture 56

W
Wakame 20
Misoshiru 110
Suimono 113
Wasabi 23, 44
Water-vinegar mixture 56

Y
Yellowjack 30, 56
Negi Shima-Aji Gunkanmaki 72
Yellowtail 30
Youfuu Oshizushi 118
Yuzu Orange 29
Karashisumiso Sauce 37
Suimono 113